With Best Wish[es]

- Donald

The Greatest BUSINESS DECISIONS of All Time

Edited by Brian Dumaine
Fortune senior editor-at-large

FORTUNE

The Greatest BUSINESS DECISIONS of All Time

HOW APPLE, FORD, IBM, ZAPPOS, AND OTHERS MADE RADICAL CHOICES THAT CHANGED THE COURSE OF BUSINESS.

By Verne Harnish and the Editors of *Fortune*
Foreword by Jim Collins

Published by *Fortune* Books, an imprint of Time Home Entertainment Inc.
135 West 50th Street
New York, New York 10020

ISBN 10: 1-60320-059-2
ISBN 13: 978-1-60320-059-2
Library of Congress Control Number: 2012935367

Fortune is a registered trademark of Time Inc.

We welcome your comments and suggestions about *Fortune* Books.
Please write to us at:
Fortune Books
Attention: Book Editors
PO Box 11016
Des Moines, IA 50336-1016

If you would like to order any of our hardcover Collector's Edition books, please call us at 1-800-327-6388 Monday through Friday, 7 a.m. to 8 p.m., or Saturday, 7 a.m. to 6 p.m. Central Time.

ACKNOWLEDGMENTS

When you delve into the great decisions chronicled in these pages, you'll find that in most instances it was the people involved that really mattered. The same holds true for producing this book. First, we want to thank *Fortune* managing editor Andy Serwer, who, displaying the vision and entrepreneurial spirit we've long admired him for, green-lighted this project in the same meeting in which we pitched it and then provided support all along the way. *Fortune* art director Emily Kehe, working with Time Inc.'s talented Anne-Michelle Gallero, applied their usual elegant sense of style to the design. Carol Gwinn, our copyeditor par excellence, used her superb language skills to save ourselves from ourselves. Steve Koepp and Joy Butts at Time Home Entertainment Inc., the book's publisher, worked creatively behind the scenes to make this project a reality, and for that we're truly grateful. And we extend our thanks and admiration to Jim Collins for providing such an insightful foreword to the book. Last, a big bow to the writers and editors on *Fortune*'s staff who used their in-depth knowledge of business and their nonpareil writing skills to make this book what I hope you'll find to be a wonderful, informative read.

**TO DECISION-MAKERS
WHO KEEP MAKING THE TOUGH CALLS**

TABLE OF CONTENTS

FOREWORD

By **JIM COLLINS**

We tend to think that decisions are very much about "what." But when I look at my research notes or at interview transcripts from the executives we've interviewed, one theme that comes through is that their greatest decisions were not "what?" but "who?" They were people decisions.

Fundamentally, the world is uncertain. Decisions are about the future and your place in the future when that future is uncertain. So what is the key thing you can do to prepare for that uncertainty? You can have the right people with you.

Let's take a nonbusiness case and a business case to illustrate the importance of the people piece. In 1978, Jim Logan and his partner, Mugs Stump, became the first people to climb the Emperor Face of Mount Robson in the Canadian Rockies. And to this day, nearly everybody else who's tried the face has either died or failed on the route. When I asked Logan, "Why were you able to do the Emperor Face?" he said, "Because I made the single most important decision, I picked the right partner."

He told me that there was this one place, the "death zone," and once they went above it, they really couldn't retreat. They were going to either summit or die—no going back. They didn't know what they were going to find beyond that point, and they didn't know what the weather was going to be. And so, therefore, what's your greatest hedge against uncertainty? Having people who can adapt to whatever the mountain throws at you.

In business, let's take the story of a company heading into a very uncertain world: Wells Fargo in the late 1970s. Everybody knows the storm of deregulation is going to hit. But nobody knows precisely how it's going to shake out. When is it going to hit? What exact form is it going to take? What impact is it going to have on the banking industry? Dick Cooley, chief executive of Wells Fargo at that time, was very clear with us when we did our research. He said, in essence, I did not know what we were going to have to do to prevail through deregulation, because it was an uncertain set of contingencies. Too many of them. But I did know that if I spent the 1970s building a team of the most capable executives possible, they would figure out what to do when deregulation hit. He couldn't lay down a plan for what was going to happen, because he didn't know what was going to happen. So his decision was actually a bunch of decisions about getting the people who could deal with whatever deregulation turned out to be.

Of course, once you have great people in place, you still have to make decisions. Great decisions begin with really great people and a simple statement: I don't know. The research evidence on that is very clear—that the leaders who ended up setting things in place that produced extraordinary results over time, and a series of great decisions over time, really were very comfortable saying "I don't know" until they knew.

And really, they were just being honest. I mean, which is best? Lying—meaning saying you don't know when you've already made up your mind? Or presuming to know when you don't and therefore lying to yourself? Or speaking the truth? Which is: "I don't yet know, but I know we have to get it right."

Typically in companies people expect the opposite. They expect their leaders to say clearly, "Here's where we're headed." The CEO has already made a decision, and his definition of leadership is to get people to participate so that they feel good about the decision he's already made.

That's wrong, because you're ignoring people who might know a lot that would be useful in making the decision. You're accepting the idea that because you're in the CEO seat, you somehow know more or you're smarter than everyone else. But what you're really doing is cutting yourself off from hearing options or ideas that might be better.

To create an atmosphere where ideas flow freely, you have to recognize that your position can be a hindrance to getting the best information. And so can your personality. My own greatest enemy is my personality—I can convince the people on my team of a point of view. I'm older than they are. I've done more research than they have. I know more than they do. I can influence them perhaps too much and therefore not get the best answers. So when we were doing the research for *Good to Great*,

I built a culture that began with disagreements, that set people up to disagree with each other and disagree with me.

I tried to increase what I call my questions-to-statements ratio. I learned this from the *Good to Great* leaders we were studying. They were just marvelous at igniting dialogue and debate with Socratic questions. And I tried to make heroes out of those on my team who identified flaws in my thinking. At the next meeting I might say, "I really want to give Leigh or Brian or Stefanie credit. She really pushed my thinking, and I wasn't looking at this right."

I looked for people with a streak of irreverence and independent thought. One of my favorite researchers is a young man who went to Princeton, majored in medieval literature, and then joined the Marine Corps. Now, that's independent thinking. I wanted him on my team because he's not going to care what I think.

The really critical part came in designing the research so that for every piece of the puzzle—for every case, every analysis—someone on the team knows that piece as well as I do or better. This was a key mechanism to reduce the odds that my authority and strong personality would override the evidence.

And I really want to underscore something. Decision-making is not about consensus. It depends on conflict, and that's the key. What we found in companies that make good decisions is the debate is real. When Colman Mockler at Gillette is trying to decide whether to go with cheaper, disposable plastic razors or more expensive ones, he asks marvelous questions. He's Socratic. He pushes people to defend their points of view. He lets the debate rage. And this is, by the way, not an isolated case. We found this process in all the companies we studied, when they made a leap to greatness. The debate is real. It is real, violent debate in search of understanding.

Then, in the end, the leader makes the call. It's conflict and debate leading to an executive decision. No major decision we've studied was ever taken at a point of unanimous agreement. There was always some disagreement in the air.

Our research showed that before a major decision, you would see significant debate. But after the decision, people would unify behind that decision to make it successful. Again, and I can't stress this too much, it all begins with having the right people—those who can debate in search of the best answers but who can then set aside their disagreements and work together for the success of the enterprise.

Creating a debate is crucial, but there are other ingredients that lead to great decisions. Most people start with the outside world and try to figure out, How do we adapt to it? Greatness doesn't happen that way. It starts with an internal drive. And there's a really key question with big decisions: What is the truth of this situation? There are three parts to this question. The first is internal: What are our real core values and our real aspirations? I mean, what do we really stand for? What do we really want to get done? What is internally driving us? I believe that it is the internal imprint that drives all the action. Everybody harps about "It's all about responding to the outside world." But the great companies are internally driven, externally aware.

So the first question is, What is really driving us internally? The second question is, What is the truth about the outside world? And in particular, What is the truth about how it operates and how it is changing?

And the third question is, When you intersect our internal drive with external reality, what's the truth about what we can distinctively contribute potentially better than anyone else in the world?

Now, let's look at Boeing's decision to build the 707. What are the factors? First, you have the values of Boeing, which had to do with "We're adventurers, for goodness' sake. We like doing big, adventurous things. We'd rather not be in business than not do that." And second, the aspiration to make Boeing even greater than it was. Those are internal drives. They had nothing to do with adapting to the outside world.

But the second question—What was the truth about the outside world and how it was changing?—well, the war was over. There wasn't going to be as much demand for bombers. And there was a major change in technology, from propellers to jets. And the demand for military aircraft was going to decline relative to demand for commercial aircraft. So that's how the outside world was changing.

On to question No. 3: What could Boeing do better than anyone else in the world? Well, they had jet technology. They'd been building those big strato bombers, the B-47 and the B-52. They had experience, so they knew they could build a large-scale jet. Boeing confronted the truth, internal and external, and grasped that it could make a distinctive impact by bringing the world into the jet age—and that's when Bill Allen pulled the trigger on the 707. (For more on Boeing's decision, see Chapter 13.)

No decision, no matter how big, is any more than a small

fraction of the total outcome. Yes, some decisions are much bigger than others; some are forks in the road. But as far as what determines outcomes, the big decisions are not like 60 of 100 points. They're more like six of 100 points. And there's a whole bunch of others that are like 0.6, or 0.006. They add up to a cumulative result. Business schools have regrettably taught us that it's all about the singular case decision.

Another big factor that affects decision-making is psychological. Do you believe that your ultimate outcomes in life are externally determined—"I came from a certain family, I got the right job"? Or do you believe that how your life turns out is ultimately up to you, that despite all the things that happen, you are ultimately responsible for your outcomes?

Consider the airline industry, and think of all the events and factors outside managerial control that have hit it since 1972: fuel shocks, interest rate spikes, deregulation, wars, and 9/11. And yet the No. 1 performing company of all publicly traded companies in terms of return to investors for the 30-year period from 1972 to 2002 is an airline. According to *Money* magazine's retrospective look in 2002, Southwest Airlines beat Intel, Wal-Mart, GE—all of them! Now what would have happened if the folks at Southwest had said, "Hey, we can't do anything great because of our environment"? You could say, "Yeah, the airline industry is terrible. Everyone in it is statistically destined to lose money." But at Southwest they say, "We are responsible for our own outcomes."

Of course, you can't entirely control your own destiny with good decisions. Luck is still a factor. But overall our research is showing that the primary factors reside more inside your control than outside. Yes, the world throws a lot at us, but the fundamental assumption needs to be like Southwest's—the ultimate responsibility for your destiny lies with you. The question is not what the world does to you but how you make an impact on the world. Decision-making is ultimately a creative act.

Our research shows one other variable to be vitally important for both the quality of decisions and their implementation. If you look at some of the great decisions in business history, the executives had the discipline to manage for the quarter-century, not the quarter. Look at Andy Grove deciding to abandon memory chips at Intel, Bill Allen and the Boeing 707, Reg Jones choosing Jack Welch to run GE, the Apple board deciding to rehire Steve Jobs, Henry Ford's decision to double the wages of his workers, Darwin Smith selling the mills at Kimberly-Clark, Jim Burke standing firm in the Tylenol crisis, Tom Watson Jr. and the IBM 360. Those leaders were very clear that their ambition was for the long-term greatness of the company.

JIM COLLINS *is the author of* Built to Last, Good to Great, How the Mighty Fall, *and* Great By Choice. *This foreword is based on the edited transcript of an interview* Fortune *conducted with Jim Collins on* Making Tough Calls.

INTRODUCTION

By **VERNE HARNISH**

THE DEATH OF STEVE JOBS gave birth to this book. Let me explain. In the fall of 2011, I was in Delhi visiting Raghoo Potini, our India partner for my firm, Gazelles, when our conversation turned to the topic of Jobs and how brilliant Apple's decision was to bring him back as CEO. (Name another major corporation where the CEO departed for a decade and was then rehired, only to bring the organization back to glory.) Ultimately that decision led to the creation—just a few months before Jobs' tragic passing—of the most valuable company in the world.

Wasn't this one of the greatest and most unlikely business decisions of all time? If so, what are the others? And wouldn't it be wonderful to get the inside story on how those industry-changing decisions were made?

A truism of life is that success equals the sum total of all the decisions one makes. And as Jim Collins suggests in the fore-word to this book, it's the combination of thousands of decisions that lead to greatness. Yet there seem to be a handful of decisions that stand apart from the rest—a few "black swan" moments, to borrow a phrase from Nassim Nicholas Taleb's groundbreak-ing book of the same name. They are often those fateful "bet the farm" moments, when a CEO can go left or right, or not go at all. And the choices great leaders end up making are often counterintuitive and move companies, industries, and even nations in entirely new directions.

Thinking over that Steve Jobs conversation during the long flight home from India, I decided it was time for someone to pull together all these important decisions. I turned to my colleagues at *Fortune* magazine, where I'm a contributor, and pitched them the idea for a book. To me, it made sense to ask writers who have long covered the companies and industries that would appear in the book to pen the chapters. They reacted with enthusiasm, and thus *The Greatest Business Decisions of All Time* was born.

Picking the best business decisions is, of course, more art than science. The search, in a sense, began some 20 years ago. At the time, I was looking for course material for an executive program I had launched in 1991 on the campus of MIT with Edward Roberts and Vince Fulmer. What the program needed, I figured, was a curriculum of insightful case studies that would appeal to the high-potential CEOs attending the program. What better way to do this than by focusing on great business decisions? Over the next two decades I started to compile a list of what I believe to be some of the best decisions made by the most successful companies in history.

In the end, the 18 management decisions that made our final list stood out from others because they were counterintuitive—they went against the grain of popular practice. Who was Andy Grove to think he could make a commodity computer chip a household name? Now we have "Intel Inside." What executive in his right mind would give his employees time to daydream—but that's exactly what 3M CEO William McKnight did in 1948.

Many of these great decisions eventually unleashed a storm of imitation—Google now lets employees spend a chunk of their time on their own projects, some 50 years after McKnight at 3M set the precedent. A few of these ideas, however, like Bill Gates' decision to take a week off once or twice a year to read and think (a habit that helped Microsoft shift its strategy a number of times) remain largely uncopied. That doesn't mean that Gates' Think Week approach might not be just the thing for some of today's business leaders. In the end, all these great decisions have stood the test of time, having created tremendous value as well as lessons for running any business.

At first we attempted to organize the decisions into various buckets. My company, Gazelles, developed a conceptual framework called the Four Decisions, which emphasizes the main categories of decisions that all companies must get right. They are: People, Strategy, Execution, and Cash. It soon became clear that it didn't make sense to stuff each decision into one of these convenient boxes. We also thought about ranking the decisions, presenting them in a reverse order like a Casey Kasem radio jock countdown of the top 40 hits, but that, too, seemed arbitrary. The only exception was naming the No. 1 greatest business decision of all time, which we save for the last chapter of the book. The harder we tried to find a way to label these wildly diverse decisions, the more we became stuck. In the end we decided to let each stand on its own merit.

Nevertheless, I do have my top five favorites. Here they are, in reverse order:

▶ **NO. 5: GENERAL ELECTRIC** Jack Welch's decision to go all-in and fund Crotonville, a first-class training center, set the tone for thousands of businesses to create corporate universities. That decision also helped develop a generation of leaders at GE who have gone on to run countless other companies.

▶ **NO. 4: SAMSUNG:** The decision by this South Korean electronics giant two decades ago to launch an unprecedented sabbatical program, placing star employees in far-flung places around the globe for a year, continues to drive Samsung's prominence as a top 20 brand.

▶ **NO. 3: WAL-MART** Sam Walton's decision to launch a simple Saturday morning meeting, for all employees, in his first store has led to 50 years of rapid decision-making, creating one of the largest companies in the world.

▶ **NO. 2: APPLE** The decision to bring back Steve Jobs as CEO of the company he founded, after a decade-long absence, resulted in "the best work of his life" and the most valuable public company in the world.

▶ **NO. 1: FORD** Henry Ford's decision to double the wages of his employees meant that workers were no longer viewed as drones, to be paid as cheaply as possible, but instead as valuable assets. In turn, workers could now afford the very products they were producing. That triggered a consumer revolution that would eventually help create the wealthiest nation on earth.

What you won't find in this book is deep or, for that matter, any analysis of the neuroscience of decision-making. For more on that topic read my colleague Luda Kopeikina's book *The Right Decision Every Time: How to Reach Perfect Clarity on Tough Decisions*. Kopeikina based her book on research she conducted on 115 CEOs. I've had her teach her techniques to the leaders in our executive program. The details of her research and that of others are beyond the scope of this book.

I also don't expect this to be the final answer on the greatest business decisions of all time. I want to spur debate on the topic. I want MBAs to wrestle with and analyze the list. I want other business leaders to validate or criticize the selections as a way for all of us to learn. Most of all, I want these decisions to ignite and inspire conversations in boardrooms and cafés about how they might apply to one's own business—and then have you share your thoughts with the rest of the world. I invite you to visit www.greatestdecisions.com to continue the debate and to nominate your own great decisions.

We hope that you enjoy the stories in the pages that follow and benefit from their shared insights.

—*Verne Harnish*

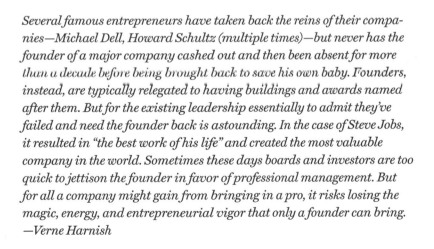

LET'S BRING BACK STEVE

By **ADAM LASHINSKY**

*Several famous entrepreneurs have taken back the reins of their compa-
nies—Michael Dell, Howard Schultz (multiple times)—but never has the
founder of a major company cashed out and then been absent for more
than a decade before being brought back to save his own baby. Founders,
instead, are typically relegated to having buildings and awards named
after them. But for the existing leadership essentially to admit they've
failed and need the founder back is astounding. In the case of Steve Jobs,
it resulted in "the best work of his life" and created the most valuable
company in the world. Sometimes these days boards and investors are too
quick to jettison the founder in favor of professional management. But
for all a company might gain from bringing in a pro, it risks losing the
magic, energy, and entrepreneurial vigor that only a founder can bring.
—Verne Harnish*

HISTORY OFTEN APPLIES a gauzy layer of film to great decisions. Take the action by the Apple board of directors in 1996 to bring back Steve Jobs to the company he had co-founded 20 years earlier. In the decade and a half between the return of Jobs and his death in 2011, Apple became the most valuable company in the world. So whoever was responsible made one hell of a good call, one of the best in business history. The facts and circumstances of Jobs' return, however, show that behind some—perhaps all—great decisions is a combination of great timing and good old-fashioned dumb luck.

It is impossible to overstate just how rotten a state of affairs Apple found itself in during its 20th year of existence— especially given the glorious narrative of its beginning. A pioneer of the personal computer, Apple had been a computer industry success story since the 1980s on the strength of its Macintosh computer. The Mac was the first consumer machine to use the straightforward icons and computer mouse that became industry standards. Under the guidance of division head Steve Jobs, the Mac was simple to use and powerfully marketed. The famous "1984" ad campaign Apple debuted at that year's Super Bowl—upstart Apple portrayed itself as the slayer of the all-powerful IBM, then the dominant force in computing—remains one of the advertising industry's proudest displays of brand and image management. By 1985, when Steve Jobs was made unwelcome at his own company by the chief executive he had personally recruited to run the place, John Sculley, Apple was wildly profitable, a market share leader, and an icon of American entrepreneurialism.

In the ensuing years, however, Apple stumbled badly. It

expanded into multiple product areas, from printers to the embarrassing Newton handheld computer. It ran a bloated supply chain, with far-flung factories and warehouses. Bloat defined its management ranks as well: Apple was a mishmash of dysfunctional fiefdoms. "Apple's stewards were trying to coast on a reputation that no longer matched up with the reality," wrote journalist Alan Deutschman in his book, *The Second Coming of Steve Jobs*. "And, arrogantly, they were demanding a premium price for products that no longer were much better, or different, from what hundreds of other PC makers were offering."

If Apple's management was weak, its board of directors wasn't much better. In 1993 it replaced CEO Sculley with Apple's German-born operations chief, a by-the-numbers executive named Michael Spindler. Facing a declining Apple, Spindler in 1995 tried peddling the computer maker to Sun Microsystems, a deal that fell apart. Around the same time software billionaire Larry Ellison, a close friend of Steve Jobs', considered buying Apple and installing his friend as CEO. Ellison never turned his talk into action, and in 1996 the board, dissatisfied with Spindler, turned to one of its own, Gil Amelio, chief executive of chipmaker National Semiconductor. Amelio essentially never had a chance at Apple. With a background selling components to other manufacturers, he had no consumer experience. He was, in Deutschman's words, "the ultimate wrong guy." Apple was outmaneuvered by Microsoft, which succeeded in making its software standard across personal computers other than Apple's. The results told the story, as Apple turned from cash gusher to money loser. In 1996, Apple lost $816 million on $9.8 billion in sales, which were heading in the wrong direction: down 11% from the previous year.

It was during this dark time that Apple's board, already guilty of botching the hiring of two CEOs, caught a break—though it nearly fumbled a third time. Amelio convinced the board that Apple needed to purchase a software company in order to gain the intellectual property and talent to replace Apple's aging operating system software. It made an offer to a company called Be, run by a former Apple executive, Jean-Louis Gassée. In a classic example of overreach, Gassée wasn't satisfied with Apple's offer, and talks between the fallen leader and the brash startup foundered. Around this time, Garrett Rice, a midlevel executive at another Silicon Valley company, NeXT, contacted a top executive at Apple with the suggestion that Apple should buy NeXT. The founder of NeXT was none other than Steve Jobs. He had started the company shortly after leaving Apple, originally as a computer maker targeting the education market. NeXT had fizzled as a hardware maker, however, and was on its way to failing in software too. Garrett had called Apple without the knowledge of Jobs, and Apple started talking to NeXT without anyone on Apple's board knowing about it. (Interestingly, Garrett left NeXT in 1997, joined Apple six years later, and remains there today.)

In late 1996 talks with Be broke down, and Apple began negotiating in earnest with NeXT, this time with Gil Amelio central to the discussion. Amelio understood the value of NeXT's software and also of the effect on morale, product vision, and creativity that could come from persuading Steve Jobs to rejoin Apple. Amelio should have been wary of Jobs. He had met with him in 1994 when Amelio joined the Apple board, and Jobs asked for Amelio's help in having himself named Apple's CEO. Then again, Amelio may have been comforted by the knowledge that Jobs had been a notoriously fractious manager in his first stint at Apple and that NeXT wasn't considered a success. Though brilliant and charismatic, Steve Jobs in 1996 wasn't obvious CEO material.

What's more, Jobs appeared to be so indifferent to rejoining Apple that he refused Amelio's request to sign an employment agreement with the company, preferring to be an informal adviser. Jobs also demanded that a large portion of the $427 million Apple paid for NeXT be paid out in cash—meaning that Jobs was less interested in the long-term incentive of ensuring a successful acquisition of NeXT than he was in getting paid. (Jobs didn't need the money at this point: The initial public offering the previous year of the computer-animation company Pixar, which Jobs controlled, had made him a billionaire.) Jobs did ask for a seat on Apple's board of directors, a request Amelio denied. The deal was announced on Dec. 20, 1996, and weeks later Jobs played a minor role in a Macworld presentation remembered mostly for a rambling, disjointed performance by Amelio.

What happened over the course of 1997 cuts to the heart of the brilliance of the decision to rehire Jobs. Amelio clearly wanted the Jobs magic at Apple, though Amelio also clearly wanted to keep his job. Yet shortly after Jobs became an "informal adviser" to his former company, he began roaming its halls as if he were the boss. It was during this time that he met Jonathan Ive, a young industrial designer who the previous year had been named Apple's chief of design. Jobs admired prototypes Ive was working on, including one for a translucent, all-in-one computer that would become the iMac. Jobs also grilled everyone he met on what he did at Apple, trying to take a measure of the place after having been gone so long.

Jobs wasn't an employee of Apple. (In fact, he was CEO of Pixar at the time.) He wasn't a significant shareholder. He wasn't even a member of the board. Yet the rumor mill around Apple began to detect a silent coup in the making. "Soon much of Silicon Valley knew that Jobs was quietly wresting power from Amelio," wrote Walter Isaacson, the biographer of Steve Jobs. "It was not so much a Machiavellian power play as it was Jobs being Jobs."

Amelio didn't help himself. He gave another rambling per-formance a month after Macworld, this time at the Apple an-nual shareholders meeting. By this time, Apple's newest board member, former DuPont CEO Edgar Woolard, became alarmed about Amelio. He discussed Amelio with Jobs as well as with senior executives at Apple. At the time Apple was in continual downsizing mode, and Woolard was concerned about the com-pany's ability to achieve its plan and also about employee mo-rale. In July, after consulting with Jobs, Woolard spearheaded a decision by the board to fire Amelio. While Woolard had no reason to be sure that Jobs would step in as CEO, he must have sensed that the organization was starting to follow the young man's lead. By firing Amelio, Woolard had made a decision that would eventually help Jobs regain power at the company. In a sense, what he decided to do—perhaps all he could do at that point—was remove any obstacles to Steve's return.

Even after Amelio had left, Jobs still was unwilling to become

CEO, partly out of concern that he couldn't be CEO of Apple and Pixar simultaneously and partly because he wasn't sure Apple would survive. Jobs did agree to join Apple's board, however, with one unusual stipulation: He wanted everyone on the board but Woolard to resign so that Jobs could remake the board with people he trusted. (Woolard persuaded Jobs to keep one other director, defense industry executive Gareth Chang, but the others all were shown the door.)

With Amelio gone, Jobs effectively began running Apple. Fred Anderson, the company's chief financial officer, became interim CEO. But Jobs was in control. He handled negotiations with Microsoft that resulted in a $150 million investment in Apple, announced in August, as well as Microsoft's commitment to continue making Microsoft Office for the Macintosh. By September, Jobs had purged the Apple board and installed a handful of friends, including Ellison and former Apple executive Bill Campbell, in their place. That month he announced that he would be "interim CEO," a title that was shorthanded around Apple as iCEO. (It is the first known instance of Apple's fetishistic use of the lower-case i.)

Jobs was back, but in a sense the board still hadn't decided to bring him back. The board hired a search firm to find a permanent CEO. But, according to someone with knowledge of the search, "nobody great would take the job at that point." Once the board had definitely decided to boot Amelio, Jobs was the only logical person to step in. Yet it's a matter of some debate years later to what extent the board sought out Jobs. "There were a fair number of us on the board who were buying NeXT to bring Steve back to the company," recalled Bernard Goldstein, an investment banker who was among those deposed from the board. "We didn't expect NeXT to bring us any technical break-through. I voted for Steve to return even though Steve made it clear to me that he didn't want me to stay."

It's a convenient storyline, but also a bit revisionist. The board members who left were most likely faced with an ultimatum: resign or lose him. Also, Jobs by this point badly wanted to be CEO of Apple again, yet he shrewdly waited for the right moment to commit. Indeed, he didn't formally drop the "i" from his title until 2000. A board that twice hired the wrong guy essentially got lucky the third time by failing to hire the right guy—but getting his services anyway. Jobs eventually would build a board of directors comprising highly accomplished individuals who nevertheless were viewed as advisers to him rather than his boss.

Interim or not, the steps Jobs took to revitalize Apple are as decisive as those of any turnaround CEO in the history of troubled companies. He moved quickly to eliminate Apple's divisional structure, choosing instead to unify decision-making, planning, and advertising around a one-company banner. He fired thousands of middle managers; hired a logistics executive—the future CEO, Tim Cook—who would shutter Apple's owned and operated factories and warehouses; and killed marginal products, including the Newton and an early digital camera, the QuickTake 150.

What made the return of Steve Jobs so compelling is how his leadership matched the culture of the company that he had founded. The employees as well as Apple's customers loved Jobs because he represented a sense of flair, showmanship, and pride that made people excited about Apple again. At a Macworld presentation in early 1998—months after taking control of Apple—Jobs showed the company's fans an exciting lineup of new computers and instilled a sense that Apple would survive. In a signature move of theatricality, he concluded his remarks and began to walk offstage, before pivoting back and saying, in a manner that reflected an afterthought: "I almost forgot. We're profitable."

The precise motivation for reinstalling Steve Jobs at Apple is irrelevant today. The fact that it happened has altered the landscape of global business for years to come.

2

HOW FREE SHIPPING SAVED ZAPPOS

By **JENNIFER REINGOLD**

During the dotcom boom, online shoe retailer Zappos was struggling to stand out in a crowded field. Then, in 1999, the founders made one desperate decision—to offer free shipping and free returns—that eventually helped the company realize that its true competitive advantage was not price, but a fanatical attention to customer service. Key to this was the notion that an online business needed to be much more than a website— that it needed to control the entire retail value chain, from warehousing to filling orders to shipping. Today much of the online industry has copied the Zappos strategy, and Internet sales are skyrocketing. A decade or so after Zappos made this crucial decision, the National Retail Federation reported that nine in 10 retailers now offer free shipping during the holiday season. It's often the simple things that break open entire industries. —V.H.

THERE'S A DEEP IRONY ABOUT momentous business decisions. It stands to reason that because they are, indeed, momentous, they would come about after intense analysis and hours or weeks of impassioned debate. Yet sometimes the opposite is true: The decisions that make or break companies are often cobbled together on the fly. Why? Because no one can come up with anything better.

That's what happened at online shoe giant Zappos in 1999, where one desperate decision—to offer free shipping and free returns—eventually helped the company realize that its true competitive advantage was not price but a fanatical attention to customer service. It would take several more years, but the seeds planted with the free-shipping decision would eventually lead Zappos to define itself not just as an online shoe company but instead as something much more grandiose: a company that just happens to sell shoes, but strives to provide the best customer service on the planet.

In 1999, however, survival was the only thing on the mind of Zappos' founder, Nick Swinmurn. It was the era of Pets.com, eToys, and even Kozmo.com, which would hand-deliver a pack of gum to your house for free. In those dotcom boom days, the scorecard was tallied by eyeballs, not profits. The same was true at Zappos—or as it was originally named, shoesite.com, which Swinmurn proclaimed would become "the Amazon of shoes." (It turned out to be a prescient call: Zappos would be acquired by Amazon in 2009 for more than $1.2 billion.) To fund his business, Swinmurn approached Tony Hsieh, a young venture capitalist who had sold his own company, LinkExchange, for $265 million. Hsieh agreed to invest—but only on the condition that Swinmurn bring on someone who actually knew shoes. So

Swinmurn hired Fred Mossler, a former shoe salesman at Nordstrom, and Hsieh agreed to fund the company for a few months until more could be raised from larger venture capital firms.

But selling shoes on the web wasn't as easy as, say, selling chewing gum. For starters, who would buy shoes without trying them on? While Zappos gained some traction, it wasn't building enough business to impress the bigger VCs, and it was fast running out of cash. How to get critical mass? According to Mossler, either Swinmurn or he (neither executive can remember who) threw out the idea of free shipping. In the ensuing conversation, someone suggested taking the risk out of returning shoes by letting a customer order several pairs, try them all on, and not be charged for doing so.

Mossler and Swinmurn had no idea how much the gambit would cost, or whether it would work—no one, to their knowledge, was offering anything similar—but it didn't much matter. They were out of options. So in November 1999 they placed a banner announcing free shipping on the top of the company's web page. They didn't even promote the free-returns part on the main site; a customer had to click through to the customer service page to see that message. "I'd like to say there was a lot of debate and analysis," says Mossler, "but there just wasn't. You just kind of went with your guts."

The guts turned out to be golden. Not only did the number of customers grow, but the conversion of customers from browsers to buyers also improved, which in turn persuaded Hsieh to continue funding the company (he became CEO in 2000). Eventually other websites also began to offer free shipping, but it was the free returns that made Zappos stand out. Customers took

41

(and continue to take) full advantage. According to Swinmurn, as many as 40% of all Zappos orders are ultimately returned. It's a huge cost—but the company views it as marketing (the only marketing cost, in fact), and the biggest returners are also the most loyal and highest-spending shoppers.

I, for one, can attest to the thrill of the UPS guy showing up at my office door with not one, but eight pairs of black boots, which I try on and model for my more fashion-forward colleagues before simply repacking the losers in the same box and sending them straight back. That convenience is why I don't shop anywhere else for shoes.

Free shipping and free returns saved Zappos. But the move was important in another way too; it caused the company to realize that its key competitive advantage was its relationship with the customer—not, as Swinmurn had originally believed, having the largest selection of shoes. That insight, in turn, informed Zappos' 2003 decision to move away from letting the shoemakers control stocking and shipping in favor of mostly holding its own inventory. Says Swinmurn: "There came a point where we realized we were not really an Internet or tech company; we were really a shoe store."

Letting the shoe companies handle fulfillment was less risky, of course, since Zappos would never have to take a hit on a thousand pairs of neon-green sneakers that no one wanted. But Hsieh realized that being able to guarantee when and how the shoes would show up at your door was as important to the customer as the return policy itself. Over a drink (Grey Goose and soda for Hsieh, beer for Mossler), they decided—again without spreadsheets or McKinsey consultants—to make yet another momentous decision.

Suddenly the virtual store was, in fact, going to be a brick-and-mortar store too, with hundreds of thousands of pairs of shoes in its warehouse. Chancy, sure, but now Zappos would control most of the interaction with the customer. After Zappos fired its logistics company and started to build its own system, cheekily called WHISKY (WareHouse Inventory System in KentuckY), sales exploded—from $1.6 million in 2000 to $8.6 million the next year and $32 million the following year. With this system Zappos could do what it wanted for its customers—including surprising some with an e-mail telling them it could ship their shoes in two days and, later, overnight rather than in a week. "The lesson," says Swinmurn, "was if you can take something standard and make it feel personalized, that's a great customer experience." One loyal customer, Hsieh wrote in his book *Delivering Happiness*, was so excited that he suggested that Zappos start its own airline.

And finally, finally, Zappos did, in fact, undergo the kind of soul-searching that all the management books say is supposed to precede a major business decision. It was 2002 and the company was growing like wildfire—though it desperately needed a line of credit to continue its expansion—but Hsieh wondered whether there was something more fundamental to discuss than cash-flow logistics or shoe brands. "Do we want to be about shoes," he wrote, "or do we want to be about something bigger?" Mossler said the company could expand into clothing and handbags. But Hsieh, who was heavily influenced by Jim Collins' *Good to Great*, had something else in mind. He said that truly great companies had a purpose that went beyond the product itself; by the end of lunch with Mossler, the two realized that the boldest move they could make would be to define the Zappos brand as about one thing only: the very best customer experience of *any* company, online or off.

Could Zappos pull it off? The three executives thought it over for more than a month and decided to go forward at a time when the company was still not profitable and its long-term survival was contingent on getting a line of credit from Wells Fargo. Despite Zappos' new logistics system and warehouse, shoemaker fulfillment still accounted for 25% of revenues. But if the trio were serious about customer service, they would have to cut the cord so that there was nothing in the supply chain they couldn't control. In March 2003, Zappos decided to end its last remaining vendor contracts and go completely on its own. Three months later Zappos received its line of credit.

And a few months after that, Hsieh, searching for a place to locate a new call center, came up with another radical decision, one with its roots planted way back in that shipping/return idea. As he wrote in *Delivering Happiness*: "To build the Zappos brand into being about the very best customer service, we needed to make sure customer service was the entire company, not just a department. We needed to move our entire headquarters from San Francisco to wherever we wanted to build out our call center." So in late 2003, Hsieh announced he was moving Zappos from San Francisco to Las Vegas—and 70 of the 90 existing employees made the move.

Today Zappos still offers free shipping. Its return policy, once 30 days, is now a full 365 days. With $1.6 billion in sales, it is a unit of Amazon, but one that has protected its zany, close-knit, cultlike culture with a passion and even its own bible—the *Zap-*

pos Culture Book. Zappos actively consults to many companies on the subject of customer service, as well as how to build lasting corporate cultures. It ranks No. 11 on *Fortune*'s Best Places to Work list and No. 3 on the NRF Foundation/American Express Customers' Choice Awards. And none of it would ever have happened were it not for that poorly researched, desperate—and deeply momentous—gut decision.

3

WHY SAMSUNG PAYS ITS STARS TO GOOF OFF

By **NICHOLAS VARCHAVER**

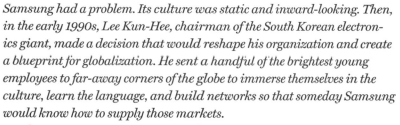

Samsung had a problem. Its culture was static and inward-looking. Then, in the early 1990s, Lee Kun-Hee, chairman of the South Korean electronics giant, made a decision that would reshape his organization and create a blueprint for globalization. He sent a handful of the brightest young employees to far-away corners of the globe to immerse themselves in the culture, learn the language, and build networks so that someday Samsung would know how to supply those markets.

What an amazing investment in the future. Today Samsung has become one of the most well-known and far-reaching brands on the planet. It's a lesson many U.S. corporations could heed. Americans are often missing in action when it comes to global business. Germany's exports per capita are almost four times higher than those of the U.S. The Netherlands government has sponsored a program somewhat similar to Lee's: It sends retired Dutch executives to countries, companies, and projects around the world. These globetrotters then source valuable opportunities for the mothership. Talk about "Act local, think global." —V.H.

STAGNATION AND INSULARITY—they're two of the most common and pernicious causes of organizational dry rot. And by the late 1980s Lee Kun-Hee began to sense just such a weakening in the foundation of South Korea's giant Samsung Group. The *chaebol*'s products were ubiquitous but uninspiring: bland copycat microwaves and electronics selling at margins even thinner than the company's microchips. Meanwhile, family management combined with a Confucian culture that venerated seniority and hierarchy made Samsung a static and inward-looking company.

In 1993, Lee, chairman of Samsung and son of the company's founder, exploded that tradition with what he called the New Management initiative. He imported Western-style employee autonomy, promotions and pay based on merit rather than seniority, and an end to lifetime tenure, along with a dramatic commitment to research and development, as part of an audacious gamble to transform Samsung into a company that designs and manufactures leading-edge technology. To say the bet paid off would be an understatement. Within a decade global revenue took off, and Samsung became an elite brand. Today, for example, its Galaxy smartphones and tablets are among the few that can compete with Apple's iPhones and iPads for coolness. By 2011, Samsung's brand ranked as the 17th most valuable in the world, according to the annual Interbrand Poll, leaving Sony—the company that defined electronics supremacy for decades—in the dust.

But it was another program that Lee launched in 1990, just ahead of the New Management initiative, that planted the seeds for Samsung's transformation. It was a simple concept: Take a handful of the company's brightest young employees, send them abroad to immerse themselves in other cultures, and then reap the benefits of increased global awareness and knowledge. The decision to launch the program was "pivotal in transforming Samsung into a global powerhouse," says Sea Jin Chang, a professor at the National University of Singapore and author of *Sony vs. Samsung: The Inside Story of the Electronics Giants' Battle for Global Supremacy.*

Since 1990 some 4,700 employees have been what Samsung calls "regional specialists," serving yearlong sabbaticals in 80 nations across the globe. "What strikes me," says Tarun Khanna, a professor at the Harvard Business School who has written about Samsung and also taught courses for its executives, "is the recognition that people steeped in Korea and speaking only Korean would require some form of unique investments to jump-start an engagement with the rest of the world."

In truth, it was hardly a new idea. As far back as the late 19th century, Japanese trading companies sent employees on training stints abroad, says Kyungmook Lee, a professor at Seoul National University, who has spent years studying Samsung. But those programs were limited in scope (typically three to six months) And, he says, most of the Japanese companies later abandoned them because they were too expensive.

Old idea or new, much of Samsung's management resisted the notion, says Kweon-taek Chung, director of the human resources and organizational research department at the Samsung Economic Research Institute. They simply didn't understand the purpose. "In the 1980s," Chung says, "going on a business trip overseas was rare in Korea, and they could not imagine sending employees abroad for a year" for something that didn't seem like work.

Even after the program launched, executives grumbled not only about the cost—close to $100,000 per specialist on top of salary and benefits for a full year—but also about the fact that the company had to give up its young stars for 15 months. They worried that the regional specialists might get recruited to other companies during their sojourns.

But chairman Lee, who wielded nearly unchecked power, brushed aside the complaints and embraced the program on a large scale during good times and bad for two decades and counting. Observes Khanna: Samsung's willingness to fund such an endeavor and its "apparently scant regard for short-term profitability concerns—even during the depths of the financial crisis—are quite unusual."

The regional specialist experience begins with what Khanna calls an "extraordinary" three-month boot camp at a massive company facility in South Korea. Much of the training consists of learning the language of the country the specialist will be living in. (That in itself was originally a big leap for a company that for decades retained the Korea-centric mindset of an operation that began as a local general store in 1938. But when Samsung began its campaign in the early 1990s, it pushed its emphasis on foreign languages far beyond the regional-specialist program. For example, the company went so far as to post English and Japanese phrases in its bathrooms, so that employees could learn even as they washed up.)

The boot camp for regional specialists includes far more than language training. There's social and physical practice too. As a 1992 article about the program described it, participants were "awakened at 5:50 for a jog, meditation, and then lessons on table manners, dancing, and avoiding sexual harassment."

From there, the regional specialists are deployed abroad for one year. In the early days many went to the U.S. and Europe; in recent years more and more have gone to emerging markets. Participating requires a measure of sacrifice: Specialists undertake the mission alone, for example, and are not allowed to bring any family members with them.

But for all the training and discipline, the biggest surprise is the free-form nature of Samsung's program—particularly in its earliest incarnation. The spirit was truly "goof off and learn." The mission was to imbibe the spirit of the country, meet people, make contacts, and write a report about what you find. That was it.

Consider Park Kwang Moo, one of the first regional specialists, whose experience was recounted in a 1992 *Wall Street Journal* article. He spent a year in the former Soviet Union, "living, eating, and drinking with Russians," learning how bribes smoothed the way for everything from airplane tickets to gasoline. "One day," the article continued, "while stoically waiting 10 hours with scores of Russians for a delayed flight, he began to understand Russia. 'I felt a strength in their misery. I felt like a Russian.'" The article went on to recount how Park's boss praised his 80-page report on the sabbatical. "There is nothing in this about business," the boss rhapsodized. "It is only about their drinking. Their idiosyncrasies. But in 20 years, if this man is representing Samsung in Moscow, he will have friends and he will be able to communicate, and then we will get the payoff."

Actually, it took a lot less than 20 years. By 2003, in an annual report that specifically credited its regional-specialist program,

Samsung proclaimed itself the bestselling brand in Russia (as well as in France and Ukraine) and claimed it had been selected as the *Narodnaya Marka*, the best national brand in Russia.

In truth, it can be hard to identify the specific achievements of the regional-specialist program, and when you do, they may seem small-bore at first glance. For example, Bill Kim, a Samsung regional specialist in Indonesia during the program's first years, told a company blog in 2011 that "an Indonesian I got to know tipped me off to unauthorized product-repair services that often led to bigger problems for consumers. Thanks to this information, we were able to provide a safer guide for consumers and modify our product designs to prevent unauthorized repairs." A 2011 cover story on Samsung in the *Harvard Business Review* co-authored by Khanna and Lee cited the regional-specialist program as fostering personal connections to key figures in various countries and a much broader understanding of local markets.

But trying to identify the concrete results misses the program's real significance. As the *HBR* article noted, it brought in fresh ideas from abroad, imparting information about other markets and corporate practices. The authors described it as "arguably the company's most important globalization effort." It nurtured a generation of managers ready to pursue Samsung's worldwide ambitions, in the view of Yongsun Paik, a professor of international business and management at Loyola Marymount University. And many of the regional specialists later get sent back to the areas they visited in senior positions at Samsung's offices there. (Interestingly, Harvard's Khanna notes that a second globalization program at Samsung, which entails bringing non-Koreans into the company in senior positions, has been much less successful. To this day few foreigners have ascended to the top ranks of the company.)

Over the years the regional-specialist program has evolved in the direction of increased control. Where once the participants could choose any area of focus, they now make the choice in close consultation with Samsung. And though it's still a yearlong program and retains its "goof-off" quotient, the free-form piece of the mission has been reduced to six months. The second six months now consists of a more applied independent project, in which participants try to learn something with tangible business utility about the market they're visiting.

Meanwhile, the program has gained stature within Samsung. Where once the selections were made by human resources officials, and line executives might carp about losing top employees for a year, now the executives themselves nominate their best candidates. That has built more management support for the program. And it has created a motivational tool that encourages competition. Young employees vie for the prestigious assignments.

The success of Samsung's program has inspired many imitators in Asia, according to Chung of the Samsung Economic Research Institute. In Korea, he says, large companies such as SK Networks, Hyundai Oilbank, Hanwha, and LG Chemical have introduced similar programs, and Korea's largest banks—Kookmin, Shinhan, and Woori—are sending bright young employees to emerging countries. In Japan, Chung says, Mitsubishi, Itochu, Sharp, and Marubeni have all introduced some version of a regional-specialist program.

Indeed, the underlying concept of exposing an organization, via its rising talent, to new markets has become so accepted today as to seem obvious. Samsung's success suggests the benefits are significant—even if they're hard to quantify. Says Harvard's Khanna of Samsung's program: "If one were ever to attempt a conventional cost-benefit analysis of some sort, I don't know whether one would decide that this was a good idea. But I would have to say that it's a brilliant idea."

THE SHAREHOLDER COMES LAST

By **TIMOTHY K. SMITH**

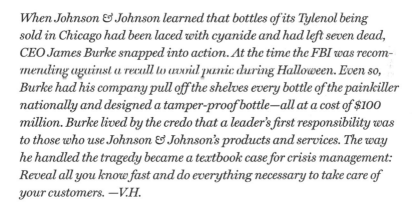

When Johnson & Johnson learned that bottles of its Tylenol being sold in Chicago had been laced with cyanide and had left seven dead, CEO James Burke snapped into action. At the time the FBI was recommending against a recall to avoid panic during Halloween. Even so, Burke had his company pull off the shelves every bottle of the painkiller nationally and designed a tamper-proof bottle—all at a cost of $100 million. Burke lived by the credo that a leader's first responsibility was to those who use Johnson & Johnson's products and services. The way he handled the tragedy became a textbook case for crisis management: Reveal all you know fast and do everything necessary to take care of your customers. —V.H.

"A FLAT PREDICTION I'LL MAKE is that you will not see the name 'Tylenol' in any form within a year," Jerry Della Femina, the Madison Avenue advertising genius, told the *New York Times* on Oct. 8, 1982. "I don't think they can ever sell another product under that name. There may be an advertising person who thinks he can solve this, and if they find him, I want to hire him, because then I want him to turn our water cooler into a wine cooler."

It was a week after an awful discovery had petrified the nation: Someone had put lethal doses of potassium cyanide into Extra Strength Tylenol capsules sold in retail stores. Seven people in the suburbs of Chicago had died. Firefighters and police officers had driven around neighborhoods with loudspeakers, warning people not to take the drug. Terrorism wasn't the term most people used for the crime in that pre-9/11 era, but the entire country was certainly terrified of Tylenol. It had been a huge hit for Johnson & Johnson—the bestselling painkiller in the U.S., with 35% of the market. But now many people shared Della Femina's judgment: Tylenol was doomed.

And yet ... it wasn't. When the *Times* spoke to Della Femina less than a year later, he said, "I was absolutely wrong. I'm really happy I was wrong." The paper noted that Compton Advertising, the agency that handled Tylenol, had sent Della Femina a water cooler filled with wine. "I drank the wine and toasted them," Della Femina said, adding, "I'm going to send them some loaves of bread. Let's see what they can do with bread."

How Johnson & Johnson saved Tylenol, and its corporate reputation, is a story that's widely regarded as the gold standard of crisis management. It was simple in conception—do the right thing, transparently—and complex in execution, involving a recall costing more than $100 million, the introduction of tamper-resistant packaging, and a gamble by the company's CEO, James E. Burke, to go before the television cameras on *60 Minutes.* One person who was present—Tom Murphy, the former CEO of Cap Cities/ABC and a Johnson & Johnson director for 20 years—says that Burke's management of the matter had its roots in a crucial decision he had made years earlier to apply the company's credo to all situations. That credo read that a leader's first responsibility was to those who use J&J's products and services. Period. By the time the crisis hit, there was no question in his mind about how to handle it. "It was no decision for him," Murphy says. "He just knew it was the right thing to do."

Thirty years later the murder case is unsolved. No one has been charged with the crime. The FBI recently reopened the investigation, hoping that advances in forensic technology and some new tips might lead somewhere. Investigators have asked a court to compel Ted Kaczynski, the imprisoned Unabomber, to provide a DNA sample (he grew up in a Chicago suburb).

For Johnson & Johnson the calamity began on Thursday, Sept. 30, 1982. The day before, two healthy people had suddenly collapsed and died, and two more had been hospitalized. A pair of off-duty firefighters, discussing the cases with each other and with paramedics, made the connection: The victims had all taken Tylenol. The firefighters alerted their superiors and the alarm was sounded, but not before more people had taken poisoned pills; the death toll was seven.

According to press reports at the time, an investigation was immediately launched at McNeil Consumer Products, the Johnson & Johnson subsidiary that manufactured Tylenol in two plants, to see whether a batch had become contaminated. Cyanide was kept at the plants for use by analytical labs. But company executives soon calculated that the amount of cyanide found in contaminated capsules—as much as 65 milligrams, well over the usual lethal dose of 50—was so high that someone would have had to dump a ton of the stuff into a batch. That and the fact that poisoned pills came from different batches, and that the deaths were clustered around Chicago, led them and the authorities to believe that someone was tampering with Tylenol bottles and leaving them on store shelves. "We have a madman out there," declared Illinois Governor James Thompson.

Burke had been at Johnson & Johnson for 30 years by then, and had been CEO for six. A marketing specialist, he had been born in Rutland, Vt., and educated at the College of the Holy Cross, the Jesuit institution in Worcester, Mass. The day after the crisis broke, Friday, he began considering a nationwide recall. Calculating a rough estimate of its cost, he came up with $100 million.

Some of his executives objected that such a recall would cause a general panic. The FBI felt the same way, according to a reconstruction of the events by Rick Atkinson in the *Kansas City Times*. Burke flew to Washington to emphasize to the agency that this was potentially a national crisis. But the FBI agents he met with resisted; they didn't want to spark a panic just a month before Halloween. Burke went over to the Food and Drug Administration to make the case for a recall to the commissioner, Arthur Hayes. While they were talking, an aide gave Dr. Hayes a note. It said that someone had found strychnine in Tylenol capsules in California. A copycat seemed to be at work.

That did it. Opposition to a recall vanished. On Tuesday the company announced that it was yanking 31 million bottles of Extra Strength capsules from stores, the biggest recall in retail history.

Burke then set up a team of seven senior executives and, according to a Defense Department study of crisis management, charged them with answering two questions: How do we protect the people? And how do we save this product?

Johnson & Johnson had been a press-shy company, but the crisis team changed that immediately. The company held press conferences, bought ads, and set up two toll-free telephone lines—one for consumers, and one with a taped daily update for news organizations.

Burke was asked for an interview by CBS's *60 Minutes*, a request that any executive in his position would dread. He sought advice from his friend Tom Murphy, who, as CEO of Capital Cities Communications, had expertise in broadcasting.

"He came to us and said, 'These people at *60 Minutes* want to do a show,'" Murphy recalls. "*60 Minutes* had a reputation for really pulverizing businessmen. All the people at Johnson & Johnson, their advertising agency, their public relations people, said, 'Don't do it, Jim, they'll just cut you up over there.'" Murphy the broadcaster knew better: He understood the value to a news program of an easy-to-understand drama with an uplifting theme. "We said *60 Minutes* is dying to do a show where they actually say something good about a businessman," Murphy says. "So we talked him into doing it, and he was a sensation." FBI director William Webster was interviewed for the show too. He said to Mike Wallace, before 10 million viewers: "The attitude of top management has been first the interest of the public, then assisting law enforcement, and then their own corporate concerns for the product."

Burke's crisis team started looking for tamper-resistant packaging. It wasn't widely used at the time, but a dozen or so types were available. A group at McNeil was assigned to try to hack them—it was known internally as Machiavelli & Co. Before long the company settled on the triple-seal arrangement that is familiar today: a foil disk under the screw cap, a shrink sleeve on the bottleneck, and a glued cardboard box.

In November, Johnson & Johnson launched a campaign to resurrect Tylenol in the new container. By then the drug's market share had fallen to about 7%. The company issued a print advertisement that read, "The makers of Tylenol want to say THANK YOU AMERICA for your continued confidence and support." It announced an offer to replace, free, any Tylenol that consumers had thrown away. It published 40 million coupons worth $2.50 toward the purchase of any Tylenol product. Burke held a satellite-linked video news conference, unusual at the time, with reporters in 30 cities. He said the company had spent about $100 million to recall, test, and destroy Tylenol in the old packaging. Calling the cyanide poisonings a "terrorist act," he said Johnson & Johnson considered it "a moral imperative, as well as good business, to restore Tylenol to its preeminent position in the market place."

It worked. Tylenol's market share was back up to 30% one year after the crimes. Noting that fact, the *New York Times* wrote, "No one may ever know who or why. But for the maker of the popular red and white capsules, at least, it is almost as if nothing ever happened."

Johnson & Johnson is one of those companies that have a credo. Written by then-chairman Robert Wood Johnson in 1943, just before the company went public, it begins, "We believe our first responsibility is to the doctors, nurses, and patients, to mothers and fathers and all others who use our products and services." In the past few years J&J's top management has seemed to ignore it, incurring so many quality-control break-downs that the company has been humiliated in congressional hearings. Burke, who retired in 1989, took it to heart, though. Management guru Jim Collins, naming Burke one of the 10 Greatest CEOs of All Time in a *Fortune* magazine article, argued that praising him for his handling of the Tylenol crisis misses the point. "Burke's real defining moment occurred three years before, when he pulled 20 key executives into a room and thumped his finger on a copy of the J&J credo," Collins wrote. "Burke worried that executives had come to view the credo as an artifact—interesting, but hardly relevant to the day-to-day challenges of American capitalism. The team sat there a bit stunned, wondering if Burke was serious. He was, and the room erupted into a debate that ended with a recommitment."

Burke's friend Tom Murphy sees it a little bit differently. "Jim would have made that decision whether the other guys believed in the credo or not," Murphy says. "He really believed in that stuff. Everyone came before the stockholders. The stockholders came last."

5

WHY DAYDREAMING PAYS OFF BIG

By **GEOFF COLVIN**

For nearly a century 3M has been one of the world's most innovative companies, creating everything from sandpaper to masking tape to Post-it Notes to DVDs. Yes, its well-financed R&D labs had a lot do with that, but more important was a decision that many of today's CEOs have lost sight of: Give your employees time to daydream. The landmark decision, made in 1948, to allow workers to spend 15% of their time on their own projects has kept the company's innovation engine humming. It led to the corollary that 30% of revenue must come from products less than five years old, a legacy that is still alive today. In 2009, even in the midst of the financial crisis, 3M launched more than 1,000 new products. Getting the most out of such a policy, however, is easier said than done. What manager wants to give up control? Here's how 3M manages its 15% rule and why some of today's most creative companies, including Google, have followed 3M's lead.
—V.H.

3M'S 15% RULE—ONE OF THE MOST FAMOUS corporate policies of any kind anywhere—has yielded billions of dollars of revenue for 3M, has helped attract inventive, ambitious employees, has strengthened 3M's corporate branding as the innovation company, and has inspired other businesses worldwide to do the same. Adopting it was clearly one of the great business decisions, yet the story behind it is widely misunderstood.

Here's how a 3M document puts it: "Regardless of their assignment, 3M technical employees are encouraged to devote up to 15% of their working hours to independent projects." Practically anyone in the business world can tell you that this rule led to the invention of Post-it Notes, a monster hit product, and many people can even tell you the story about the 3M scientist whose bookmarks kept falling out of his hymnal at choir practice, inspiring him to develop the idea and the technology for the product.

It's a wonderful story, and it's sort of true. But it's also misleading about how that innovation actually happened and about how things generally happen at 3M.

Note that the 15% rule isn't a rule. It doesn't require anyone to do anything. It just says that technical employees are allowed and encouraged to spend 15% of their time on whatever strikes their fancy. So let's call it a policy rather than a rule.

Enormous value derives not from its being a mandate that was handed down by a CEO but rather from its being a central element of the culture that goes back to the company's early days. It's important not because someone had the brilliant idea of propounding it but because it was present in the air everyone breathed.

And while the 15% policy evolved, calling it a great business decision is still correct. It had to be allowed and then encouraged to evolve, and in 3M's early decades that took courage. The company struggled. Even when it gained its footing, it was up against giant competitors. Every manager's instinct in those circumstances is to clamp down and exert more control, yet 3M's leaders did the opposite. Any of 3M's CEOs could have quietly rescinded the policy, and the temptation must have been great in tough times; the dollar benefits would have been immediate, and no one would ever have known for sure what had been lost. Yet every CEO has resisted.

Stating the policy formally, as CEO William McKnight did in 1948, was a key element of this great decision. Making the policy official—and, critically, including the specific 15% figure—turned it into something that outsiders would notice and talk about. It also lent a useful distinction to a company that increasingly proclaimed its innovativeness. A skeptical customer or investor might ask, Why should I believe 3M is any more innovative than another company? The explicit 15% policy was a reason.

The policy's fame came long after it was a de facto reality at 3M. In explaining how it came to be, one could say that this company was always on the lookout for new ideas. Or one could say that 3M was started by people who had absolutely no idea what they were doing. Both explanations are valid.

The most striking feature of 3M's early history is its founders' utter cluelessness and recklessness. In 1902 five businessmen from the northern Minnesota village of Two Harbors called their new company Minnesota Mining & Manufacturing, hinting at trouble from the beginning—none of them had any background in mining or manufacturing. But the area was booming as iron ore and other minerals were being discovered nearby. 3M's founders intended to mine corundum, a super-hard mineral that could be used to make grinding wheels. After two years of work and investment, they found that their mineral wasn't corundum; it was anorthosite, a softer material that was terrible for making grinding wheels. The founders gave up on selling the mineral and decided to start manufacturing grinding wheels themselves, a business of which they were entirely ignorant. That didn't work out. So they turned their focus to making sandpaper, another business they knew nothing about.

The one fortunate result of their repeated failures was that they were forced to find a new investor, a successful entrepreneur who supplied cash and eventually took over as president. He knew nothing about sandpaper either but was shrewder than the founders and guided the company to its first profitable product, an abrasive cloth that led 3M to the sandpaper business. Getting there had taken 12 years.

The company progressed slowly. In the early 1920s a young employee, an engineering school dropout named Richard Drew, was delivering new sandpaper samples to a local auto-body shop for testing. He heard workers raging over the lousy tape they used to mask areas for painting; when removed, it took paint off or left adhesive on the car. Drew promised them he'd invent something better, though he had no idea how. After weeks of work, his boss told him to knock it off and get back to work on sandpaper. Drew kept developing the tape when he could sneak the time. The result, introduced in 1925, was masking tape, one of 3M's all-time hit products.

We can see the forces shaping 3M's culture. Almost from day one, the company was searching obsessively for new ways to make money. It didn't just want new products; it desperately needed them to stay alive. And when an employee defied his boss to work on a product he was passionate about, he produced a major success.

Crucially, Drew's boss was William McKnight, the future CEO who was then general manager. That experience in particular, the masking tape story, changed McKnight's view about managing researchers. That's when the 15% policy began, long before it was formalized or named.

Adopting it was far riskier and braver than it appears today. Giving employees such freedom not only surrendered managerial control but also directly contradicted the leading business wisdom. It was the heyday of Taylorism, scientific management, time and motion studies. Employees weren't humans; they were moving parts in a giant machine, and the last thing you wanted them to do was think. Frederick Taylor was brutally clear: One of the first requirements for an ironworker, he wrote, "is that he shall be so stupid and so phlegmatic that he more nearly resembles in his mental makeup the ox than any other type." And it was hard to say Taylor was wrong. His methods increased productivity so enormously, Peter Drucker has observed, that our prosperity today is simply unimaginable without him. Drucker has even called Taylor's thinking "the most lasting contribution America has made to Western thought since *The Federalist Papers.*"

Who would dare to say such thinking is plain wrong? Yet McKnight and 3M's other leaders in the 1920s and 1930s realized that industrial researchers were a different breed, what we now call knowledge workers, who are best managed by different rules. Rigorous studies of creativity and innovation have blossomed in recent decades, and they strikingly validate what 3M's leaders figured out through experience, or just intuited.

The central finding is that most of the time intrinsic motivation is stronger than extrinsic motivation in sparking creativity and innovation. Highly creative people are focused on the task, not on themselves. They're asking, How can I solve this problem?, and not What will solving this problem do for me? Trying to push creative people doesn't work. They aren't pushed; they're driven.

The finding holds up strongly any way you look at it. People who score highly on tests of intrinsic motivation consistently produce work that in studies is judged more creative. Conversely, people like artists and research scientists, who work in professions that demand creativity, reliably score highly on tests of intrinsic motivation.

The research findings sound like common sense, but they go further. Many studies have found that when people expect their work to be judged by others, it is less creative than if they're doing it solely for themselves. Even knowing that they're being watched results in less creativity. 3M's leaders seemed to understand all of that years before social scientists proved it.

They also seemed to understand a more surprising finding: When people are offered a reward for doing the work, they're sometimes less creative—that is, introducing extrinsic motivation can actually reduce innovation. But it need not be so. Research has also found that the right kind of extrinsic motivators can increase innovation. Specifically, the expectation of being recognized and getting constructive, nonthreatening feedback can motivate innovative people. 3M introduced those motivators long ago, establishing the Carlton Society, named after an early research chief, to honor the company's most distinguished scientists. In 1951 it created the 3M Technical Forum, a voluntary organization where scientists could present their ideas and ask for advice. Those institutions furnish recognition and helpful feedback—exactly what excellent research scientists really value.

In practice, the 15% policy is mushier than that precise 15% number might suggest. For research scientists, as for most knowledge workers, the distinction between personal time and working time doesn't mean much and never did. A company publication quotes an early researcher recalling an era long before the 15% policy was enunciated: "People in Central Research were on their honor when it came to working hours. If a guy decided to go fishing on a weekday, Carlton knew the time would be made up. If he decided to work independently on his own product idea, he had the freedom to do it—even if the boss said otherwise." On the other hand, then as now, if a deadline has to be met, your first responsibility is to meet it; do your 15% time some other time.

The 15% rule also allowed 3M to make other conscious decisions that enhance its core competency—innovation. One notable example is its Innovation Center in Austin, which to this day provides employees with not only the time but also the space for innovating. The center itself is designed creatively. It has, for instance, reflective roof panels that maximize direct sunlight into the facility. The break rooms and restrooms are located in such a way that various functions bump into each other. Other specially designed rooms facilitate spontaneous innovation sessions.

The 15% policy has paid 3M richly. Sometimes it has yielded famous products, like Scotchgard fabric protector and Micropore medical tape. Sometimes it has led to inventions the public has never heard of, such as a machine that improved the tape-manufacturing process and saves the company millions of dollars a year.

As for Post-it Notes, the critical discovery—an adhesive that stuck to paper and other surfaces yet could be removed without damaging them—was made by senior scientist Spencer Silver as part of his normal work, not a personal project. No one in the company saw a use for it. Five years later scientist Art Fry had his eureka moment with bookmarks in his hymnal. He ordered some of the adhesive and started applying it to paper. The results looked promising, but the technical challenges of getting the adhesive right and coating paper precisely were huge. He did spend some 15% time working on them, but it was no renegade project; his boss also gave him time and money. So don't credit Post-it Notes to the 15% policy. Do credit them to the culture.

The 15% policy has inspired other companies to imitate it directly. Most famously, Google gives engineers 20% of their time to pursue their own projects; so do Atlassian, an Australian software firm, and some smaller outfits. More broadly, 3M's decision showed a doubtful world one of the knowledge economy's most important and counterintuitive principles: A company can improve its performance by giving up control.

6

HOW INTEL GOT CONSUMERS TO LOVE CHIPS

By **DAVID A. KAPLAN**

It would be fun to imagine the meeting where young assistant Dennis Carter suggested to CEO Andy Grove that Intel spend what would eventually amount to billions on an ad campaign to brand its computer chip with the general consumer: But, Dennis, we can name our direct customers on one hand. Why do we need an expensive consumer ad campaign that highlights a component that most people don't understand or really care about? Have you been smoking something? Anyway, the rest is history—Intel is one of the most recognized consumer brands in the world. More important, creating the "Intel Inside" campaign was a critical decision in preventing the commoditization of the computer chip. Consumers could be made to care about the chip inside their computer. In Michael Porter's five-forces analysis, Intel's move created what he might call a major shift in power. Other companies have discovered that an anonymous ingredient of a larger consumer product might achieve its own identity—consider what NutraSweet, Teflon, and Dolby have all accomplished. —V.H.

PCs ARE MADE OF VARIOUS COMPONENTS: the case, power unit, keyboard, mouse, hard disk, videocard, motherboard, and—the brains of the operation—the microprocessor. Way back when, users of a Compaq no more knew who had supplied those ingredients than a Chevy owner knew who had made the radiator under the hood. "Quick, name your favorite microprocessor!" was likely to make people at a cocktail party conclude you were a geek—and then to flee. Intel changed all that in 1991. Until then, the high-tech marketing landscape had pretty much consisted of Apple's rainbow logo and IBM's Little Tramp. But if a small blue Chiquita sticker could turn a banana into a marketing icon, then why not an Intel Inside logo on a computer? Even better, why not add a modest jingle that would become a legend?

Those were the ideas behind Intel's decision to talk directly to consumers about its microprocessors—a revolutionary marketing strategy that would transform Intel, the maker of an entirely unsexy commodity, into one of the most recognized brands in the world. In a range of rankings over the past decade and a half, Intel has been considered right up there with the likes of Coke, McDonald's, and Disney. Many computer users today, boasts an Intel corporate history, "can recite the specification and speed of the processor, just like car owners can tell you if they have a V4, V6, or V8 engine." Worldwide, as part of a gigantic "cooperative" marketing program, thousands of PC makers now license the Intel Inside logo, helping to sell their own products—along with Intel's. How the Intel Inside campaign happened is a story of instinct and nerve, luck and execution.

Intel has long been a Silicon Valley behemoth. Founded in 1968 by Gordon Moore and Bob Noyce, Intel—its name was a play on "integrated" and "electronics"—aimed to be the leader in developing semiconductor memory for mainframes and mini-computers, which were entirely the tools of business. With the ascendance of the personal computer beginning in the early 1980s—as companies like Apple and Microsoft and Dell Computer blossomed—Intel's business model came to focus on PCs. In 1980, Intel won the contract for IBM's heralded entry into the market, and by the mid-1980s the company had two-thirds of the overall market for desktop microprocessors (or "chips"). In 2011, with nearly $44 billion in annual revenue, Intel ranked No. 56 on the *Fortune* 500.

The genesis for Intel Inside came in 1988 from inside the cubicle of CEO Andy Grove. His young technical assistant, Dennis Carter—who had two engineering degrees, as well as an MBA from Harvard Business School—understood that the company faced challenges in the maturing microprocessor market. The surprising cause: the very success of the microprocessor. Because of Moore's Law (named after the Intel co-founder)—which holds that the number of transistors on a microprocessor roughly double every 18 to 24 months—Intel and other chip manufacturers were able to quickly make obsolescent each generation of chip. So Intel's 16-bit microprocessor—called the 286—was replaced within three years by the 386, a 32-bit microprocessor.

Trouble was, "nobody was buying it," according to Carter in a 2002 Harvard Business School case study, "Inside Intel Inside." "Everybody was still wedded to our 286 chip. The 386 was a much better product, but it had only been adopted in high-end products such as servers. PC manufacturers weren't yet displacing the 286." That was "particularly troublesome," wrote the author of the case study, professor Youngme Moon, since Intel "was now on the verge of launching its fourth-generation microprocessor, the 486 chip." Carter hypothesized that Intel's strategic problem was one of marketing rather design. "In the past, we had always focused our energy on marketing" to engineers at the computer manufacturers themselves. But as the number of consumers swelled and as less sophisticated IT managers took over decision-making for which PCs companies should buy, "design engineers didn't have the same clout anymore," Carter told Moon.

Carter wondered whether "maybe the problem was that end users weren't aware of the product differences." If he was correct, the solution was to reach those consumers and try to explain both that faster chips in fact produced superior performance and that Intel's faster chips were better than the competition's. He proposed a marketing test. Appealing directly to customers had a bad name at Intel. In the early days of the company it briefly had entered the digital-watch business. Marketing folks made an expensive proposed TV ad that starred Arte Johnson, of *Rowan & Martin's Laugh-In*. The ad was so bad it never aired—and, according to Carter, "it left a bad taste in Intel management's mouth about end users." Grove had his own practical concerns. "We're not structured" for it, he told his technical assistant. Carter persisted. "And Andy sort of threw me out of his office," according to Carter's account in a 2004 oral history for Stanford University Libraries. But Grove in early 1989 agreed to the test, telling Carter, "You believe it—you go do it." While Grove promised a total budget of $5 million, he told Carter, "Spend a tenth of that, and if you prove your thesis, you can spend the rest."

With a small team at Intel, Carter first conducted enough market research to confirm that consumers indeed had the mistaken view that the 386 chip was unnecessary—that the 286 was perfectly adequate and that the 386 might even present issues of software incompatibility. Then, with an ad agency, he chose a single market to take his $500,000 budget slice and see whether he could alter consumer misperceptions in a six-week campaign. Denver provided relatively cheap, accessible media: billboards. An adman aptly named Chip Shafer came up with the elegant concept called Red X: a big, bold "286" inside a circle, with a large red "X" spray-painted over the "286." After a couple of weeks, another sign went up next it: a "386" inside a circle. A blitz of newspaper ads augmented the billboards. The message was clear, and those buying PCs got it: Sales of computers with Intel's 386 microprocessor shot up. Subsequent research among buyers underscored that it was the ads that had converted opinions. It was a major moment: Carter had shifted power in the microprocessor industry from the PC makers to a key supplier.

Some at the company were horrified that in promoting the 386 the billboards had to disparage another Intel product. But Carter carried the day. "Luckily our Red X campaign was successful not only in Denver but the other cities as well," he recalled in the Harvard case study. "By the time our test was completed, we'd created a bit of excitement in the company because it had worked." Grove was impressed. Carter became head of marketing. He had demonstrated that an anonymous ingredient of a larger consumer product might achieve its own identity—akin to what NutraSweet, Teflon, and Dolby had accomplished.

The 386 drove the 286 into the ground—and then quickly

came the 486. Carter understood that branding individual, evanescent microprocessors was a fool's errand. (There was also the problem of court rulings holding that mere numbers, like 286 or 386, could not be trademarked, so risk existed that ads for a PC with such a microprocessor might wind up benefiting competitors like AMD with comparable chips.) Instead, Intel needed "an umbrella brand" to cover any iteration of chip. "We're all engineers," he told Moon, "so we approached the challenge by doing lots of research. Our research showed that 'Intel' was the best name. We then had several ad agencies give us proposals for taglines, and we ended up choosing a dark-horse candidate because we really liked "Intel. The Computer Inside."

Even so, that tagline risked alienating the actual PC manufacturers. "I could predict their initial reaction," he recalled in the case study. "If Intel is the computer, then what are we?" The way out was cooperative advertising, in which the PC manufacturers could build up credits for advertising dollars based on how many Intel microprocessors they bought. When the manufacturer ran ads, it could recoup from Intel up to half the cost via the credits. All manufacturers had to do was put Intel's logo on the bezel of the PC and in any ads. Intel Inside became the logo. Intel and the manufacturers were now in it together. Tech columnists were certain the plan would fail. Tech columnists were wrong. Dell signed on immediately—as did hundreds more by the end of 1991. An early print ad in the *Wall Street Journal* showed just how shrewd the co-op system worked. While IBM took out the ad (for its PS/2)—one horse chasing the tail of another—the Intel Inside swirl got equal billing with IBM.

The swirl in the *Journal* was black. But eventually it was replaced in ads with the distinctive blue that endures today, though Intel has allowed color variation. Intel's own "How to Spot the Very Best Computers" ad showed an array of differently colored Intel Inside swirls across the page. "It's really quite easy," consumers were told in what became known as the "measles" ad. "Just look for computers that have a genuine Intel microprocessor inside. Either the Intel386, Intel386 SX, Intel386 SL, Intel486, or Intel486 SX. With Intel inside, you know you've got unquestioned compatibility and unparalleled quality." It wasn't the stuff of Coke polar bears or Pepsi puppies, but it got the job done.

TV was the obvious next step. Intel hired George Lucas' cinematic special-effects shop, Industrial Light & Magic, to make a spot. Done in the style of *Fantastic Voyage,* the slick ad did a dramatic fly-through inside a PC's circuitry and wound up hovering over the microprocessor. "It was very visible and got the marketplace's attention," Carter said in his Stanford oral history. "That went a long way to really establishing the Intel image." In 1992, the first full year of Intel Inside, sales worldwide increased 63%. In Europe, for example, brand awareness among PC buyers rose from 24% to 94% by 1995. For a time Intel stuffed "bunnies" were a collectible toy, and Bunny People—colorfully dressed Intel fabrication plant employees dancing to a pulsating '70s disco—appeared in a 1997 Super Bowl ad. "Nothing less than the whimsical icons of a go-go PC industry," declared *Advertising Age.* The ubiquity of the Intel Inside brand may have been best symbolized by the gigantic blue swirl emblazoned on the sixth-floor rooftop of Intel headquarters in Silicon Valley until 2002, when reroofing eliminated it.

But it was a three-second, five-note jingle, or what Intel calls "the bong"—that became Intel's signature attribute in the mid-1990s. Played at the end or the beginning of every TV and radio co-op program ad, the instantly identifiable jingle energized the Intel brand. Though it's gone through some modifications over the years, the notes remain the same: D-D-G-D-A (written by Walter Werzowa from the 1980s Austrian band Edelweiss). If there's a more hypnotic, annoying jingle—yes, we're well aware of "Meow Meow Meow Meow," performed by a singing cat—we don't know of it.

The iconic brand that was launched in 1991 endures. In the years since, billions have been spent by Intel and its co-op partners on advertising. Billions of Intel Inside stickers have been put on PCs and elsewhere. Intel Inside has been supplemented with such recognizable chip names as Pentium, so consumers could know what to look for at Best Buy or online at Dell. Intel's chip never was commoditized. The company's share of the microprocessor market has stayed near 80%. Intel surely makes a solid product. So do its competitors. Intel can tout its "safety" and "reliability" and "quality" for all time. What truly separated Intel from the pack—long after it got started in the world of high tech—was a little swirl and a bong.

7

JACK'S CATHEDRAL

By DAVID A. KAPLAN

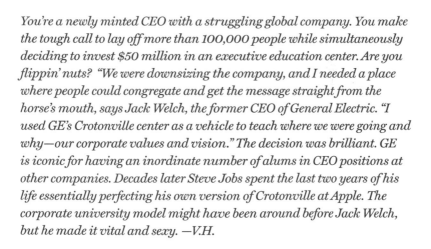

You're a newly minted CEO with a struggling global company. You make the tough call to lay off more than 100,000 people while simultaneously deciding to invest $50 million in an executive education center. Are you flippin' nuts? "We were downsizing the company, and I needed a place where people could congregate and get the message straight from the horse's mouth, says Jack Welch, the former CEO of General Electric. "I used GE's Crotonville center as a vehicle to teach where we were going and why—our corporate values and vision." The decision was brilliant. GE is iconic for having an inordinate number of alums in CEO positions at other companies. Decades later Steve Jobs spent the last two years of his life essentially perfecting his own version of Crotonville at Apple. The corporate university model might have been around before Jack Welch, but he made it vital and sexy. —V.H.

IN EARLY 1981, JACK WELCH wasn't yet known as "Neutron Jack" or the "Most Admired CEO in the World." At 45, after years ascending the company's corporate ladder, he was just starting out as General Electric's youngest chairman and CEO. He immediately stood out. In deciding to lay off thousands and restructure the company in his confrontational style, Welch transformed General Electric. But he also made a decision little-noticed at the time that would wind up influencing his entire 20-year reign. He resolved to create a world-class internal business school for GE managers. Best known as Crotonville, because of its location in a hamlet of the same name in the New York suburbs north of Manhattan, the school is now an essential part of Welch's legacy.

It didn't start out that way. Crotonville was founded by former CEO Ralph Cordiner in 1956—just a few miles away from the notorious Sing Sing Correctional Facility in Ossining, N.Y. The 53-acre retreat was designed to foster decentralization. As Welch himself explained it in his memoir, *Jack: Straight From the Gut*, "Thousands of GE managers were taught to take control of their own operations with profit-and-loss responsibility." It worked well for a long time. Instructors at Crotonville taught courses based on GE's Blue Books, which were thousands of pages of do's and don'ts. "Back in those days, the POIM (Plan-Organize-Integrate-Measure) principles spelled out in the Blue Books were like commandments," recalled Welch, who arrived at GE in 1960 as a $10,500-a-year chemical engineer fresh out of the University of Illinois at Urbana-Champaign. "But once decentralization took hold, Crotonville was used less as a training ground for leadership development" and more as merely a forum for delivering technical instruction or companywide messages.

By the time Welch took over at GE, Crotonville wasn't seen as a nonpareil proving ground for executive talent. Anybody could sign up for its programs—including those Welch called "the tired ones looking for a last reward." No longer were GE's rising stars the only ones to attend. Welch thought Crotonville "was tired—real tired." He had been one of seven contenders to become CEO—and hadn't bothered to attend a multiweek course on general management. In an earlier time not attending might have been unheard-of. Welch had one other bugaboo about Crotonville: Based on the single one-week marketing class he had taken there in the late 1960s, he remembered that the accommodations, well, stank. "Managers were being housed in barren quarters, four to a suite," Welch lamented in his memoir. "The bedrooms had the feel of a roadside motel. We needed to make our own people and our customers who came to Crotonville feel that they were working for and dealing with a world-class company."

So he set out to shake things up—at Crotonville, as at the entire company, whose traditional ways had produced torpor and complacency. Barely two weeks into his administration, Welch went to Jim Baughman, a former professor from the Harvard Business School who was running Crotonville. "We're going to be making all kinds of changes in this company," Welch told him, "and I need Crotonville to be a big part of it." Welch thought Crotonville would provide the vehicle to get his messages out to key executives "in an open give-and-take environment"—"the perfect place to break through the hierarchy."

"We were going through radical change," Welch told me in an

interview for this book. "We had become a bloated bureaucracy, and we had too many layers and filters on the message. We were downsizing the company, and I needed a place where people could congregate and get the message straight from the horse's mouth. I used it as a vehicle to teach where we were going and why: our corporate values and vision."

That was a view consistent with the center's origins, but Welch believed the faculty, the curriculum, and the atmosphere all had to be overhauled. The first step: Fix the physical plant. Welch committed nearly $50 million to modernize Crotonville over the course of the decade: a new residence center; a new "Pit," the well of a brightly lit multilevel classroom center; and a helipad, so that Welch and others could whiz in from corporate headquarters, otherwise an hour's car ride away in suburban Connecticut or Manhattan. When Baughman gave Welch a chart-filled preview of his presentation to the GE board of directors, Welch replaced the specific "payback analysis" figure on the last chart with the word "INFINITE" to underscore Welch's belief in the limitless ROI for Crotonville.

The decision to remake Crotonville naturally had its critics. It didn't help Welch that he was producing plenty of grist for the "Neutron Jack" mill. Within a few years of his taking charge, about 25% of the GE workforce was sent packing—more than 100,000 people. By his own admission, Welch was "adding fuel to the fire" by investing millions in items he acknowledged some might call "nonproductive," like a gym at headquarters. The Crotonville upgrade fit into that narrative, and critics within GE took to calling the resplendent new digs "Jack's Cathedral." The high priest was unrepentant. "You can't aim to be the best company in the world with cinderblock cells," Welch told me. "You had to have a beautiful symbol of excellence."

Once Crotonville's facilities became first-class, Welch demanded the same for its students. Attendance would now be by invitation only. Crotonville had become a place where you put people who could afford to be away from work for a few weeks," Welch said. "It was not a prized assignment to be 'sent up the river.' I wanted it to become a place where the reaction around the company was, "Ohmigod, *he* got selected?!" (Let it be said that Jack Welch was never shy about fomenting competition inside GE.)

What actually went on at Crotonville, in the classrooms and beyond, revolutionized the company. While there still were the standard array of functional courses, ranging from new-employee orientation to marketing and finance, the crucial part of the curriculum centered conceptually on leadership. The faculty created three levels of leadership courses, each running three weeks: the Management Development Course (MDC) for potential stars who were early in their careers, the Business Management Course (BMC) for midlevel managers, and the Executive Development Course (EDC), for those Welch said had "high-potential characteristics." The EDC was so exclusive that nobody could go without approval from the head of human resources, the vice chairmen, and Welch. The "faculty" was made up of GE outsiders, like regular faculty members from Harvard and other elite business schools, though increasingly GE executives themselves taught at least part of the courses. Similarly, while case studies—the bedrock of an MBA curriculum—were used, they were increasingly based on issues at GE rather than at other large companies.

The MDC was offered roughly six to eight times a year. With up to 100 students in each class, it was taught entirely at Crotonville. The two higher-level courses used what Crotonville called "action learning," which tended to concentrate on a single topic, like quality control, or a single country. Sometimes the classes took place in that country. For example, on the day the Berlin Wall came down, GE was teaching the BMC there. The BMC was offered three times a year and had 60 managers per class. The EDC was taught but once annually and had three to four dozen of GE's best and brightest. Both the BMC and the EDC culminated in a presentation of recommendations to Welch and other top executives. That was one way the participants came to understand how seriously the brain trust took Crotonville. Today, 90% of GE's top 600 managers are promoted from within.

Welch and others viewed Crotonville's managers qua students as in-house consultants. "They evaluated how fast and effective" GE's new initiatives were doing, Welch said in *Straight From the Gut.* "In every case, there were real takeaways that led to action in a GE business. Not only did we get great consulting by our best insiders, who really cared, but the classes built cross-business friendships that could last a lifetime."

By the 1990s, according to Welch, Crotonville had completely turned around, and was "an energy center, powering the exchange of ideas." Teachers saw in the classroom that they were getting the best students GE had to offer, and the students themselves—in part because of the very fact they had been invited—bought into the notion of an in-house corporate university, much as they had when Crotonville began.

Crotonville also began inviting in major GE customers, both to offer ideas about "best practices" and to listen to GE's ideas about them. For prospective customers, such coveted access might be why GE ended up getting a deal over a competitor offering similar prices. Steve Kerr, who at one point ran Crotonville for GE, recalled that when a customer was deciding between, say, GE Plastic and ABC Plastic, where price and availability were basically equivalent, the trump card GE played was Crotonville. Kerr says the sales conversation would go like this: "If you purchase GE Plastic, we'll throw in some tickets for your leadership team to participate in the highly coveted Crotonville education center. After all, it's not about the plastic, it's about helping you become a better leader so you succeed."

Eventually the faculty became dominated by GE insiders, in large part because Welch read in *Fortune* that Roger Enrico at Pepsi was teaching leadership courses to his executives. These days the vast majority of Crotonville teachers come from GE. The main attraction for years was Welch. Though he had a Ph.D. and once considered the university life, he had been an executive his whole career. Even so, he fancied himself a teacher and early on often informally taught those at GE. One technician, Pete Jones, needed math help to get a degree. In Welch's office in Pittsfield, Mass., he tutored Jones—and if Jones wasn't picking things up fast enough on the blackboard, Welch threw chalk on him. Jones would go on to a 30-year career teaching in the local school system. Welch loved being in the Pit at Crotonville, where several times a month he held forth for four hours or more. He would usually arrive near the end of a three-week course, after other teachers had primed the audience to duel with Welch.

"It was one of my favorite parts of the job," he recalled in his memoir, noting that he taught roughly 18,000 students in 21 years. "Going there always rejuvenated me." Welch's MO wasn't lecturing but engaging in a give-and-take, though it took a decade before the students developed enough gumption to do as much "giving" as the CEO. Before class, he would often arrange to have distributed a handwritten memo of his agenda. For one MDC, reproduced in his memoir, he wanted to cover "What are the major frustrations you deal with on a daily basis?" and "What don't you like about a career in GE that you would like to see changed?" In the EDC class, he asked what would they do "if they were appointed CEO of GE tomorrow," which a few of them aimed for, if not tomorrow, then one day. One manager, Jeff Immelt, did go on to succeed Welch (though Welch can't recall whether Immelt ever answered the question in class). Sometimes the class would cover a recent management or ethical dilemma, like how to fire an employee or whether to close a domestic plant—and sometimes the line executive was even there to explain a decision. Those were "rich" and "personal" discussions, Welch wrote. "Everyone in the room left knowing they weren't alone in facing a tough call."

After a full day in the Pit, Welch met students in the rec center for drinks and more debate. Over time students appreciated that they were hearing about GE strategy straight from the boss, which was not always the same line they were hearing from superiors back home. Any large organization struggles with the disconnect between the message given out at the top and the message as it's filtered by those with their own agenda or merely a bad ear. Initially that bureaucratic disconnect—Welch called it "pockets of resistance"—led to confusion and annoyance among the students. Eventually, though, Crotonville succeeded wildly in giving the CEO of a multinational colossus a convincing, authentic way to solve that disconnect.

Welch used the liberating dynamic of Crotonville—openness, directness, responsiveness—to create Work-Out meetings at various corporate locations. "Coaching" and "listening," rather than "preaching" and "controlling," were the watchwords. During a session lasting a few days, prompted by outside "facilitators," groups of 40 to 100 lower-level employees got to vent their spleens—in the service of taking unnecessary work out of the GE system. The best part may have been that managers who attended the sessions had to give yes-or-no decisions on the spot for at least 75% of the ideas suggested; if they couldn't decide, they had to give a date for resolution.

Whereas over the years tens of thousands have made it to Crotonville, hundreds of thousands began participating in Work-Outs and other training that were inspired by the lessons of Crotonville. Many programs are in the U.S., but a number of others are in such places as Shanghai, Munich, Abu Dhabi, Brussels, New Delhi, and Mozambique. "Small wonder that people began to forget their roles," Welch wrote. "They started speaking up everywhere." A GE appliance worker put it bluntly to Welch: "For 25 years you've paid for my hands when you could have had my brain as well—for nothing."

That is what was wrought by Crotonville, which was aptly rechristened the John F. Welch Leadership Development Center. As of 2012, some 10,000 students come through its doors each year. Half are from abroad. The GE Women's Network puts on a Leading & Learning summit for 150 women leaders.

A "journey to Crotonville," boasts the GE mantra, "is something of a pilgrimage—a transformative learning experience that, for many, can become a defining career event."

Crotonville's cultural legacy extends beyond its corporate boundaries. None other than Apple seems to be trying to emulate it. Inspired in part by how "the HP Way" proved to be Bill Hewlett and Dave Packard's most enduring contribution to the Silicon Valley canon (see Chapter 17), Steve Jobs spent part of his final years aiming to perfect his own version of Crotonville: Apple University, a secret executive-training program that would institutionalize the surely idiosyncratic gifts of the late, great co-founder.

Shocking the world of academe, Jobs in 2009 convinced Joel Podolny to leave the deanship of the Yale School of Management to build it. Podolny's job is somehow to put together a curriculum of people and ideas and written materials to show Apple managers how to thrive, even if they could never—and should never—seek to think as Jobs would have. Such is a formidable, perhaps impossible, task. Before GE and Jack Welch made the corporate-university model vital and sexy, it would have been an unthinkable assignment.

8

BILL GATES DECIDES TO TAKE A WEEK OFF

By DAVID A. KAPLAN

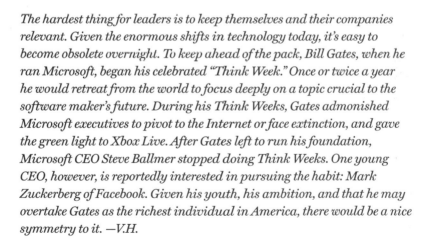

The hardest thing for leaders is to keep themselves and their companies relevant. Given the enormous shifts in technology today, it's easy to become obsolete overnight. To keep ahead of the pack, Bill Gates, when he ran Microsoft, began his celebrated "Think Week." Once or twice a year he would retreat from the world to focus deeply on a topic crucial to the software maker's future. During his Think Weeks, Gates admonished Microsoft executives to pivot to the Internet or face extinction, and gave the green light to Xbox Live. After Gates left to run his foundation, Microsoft CEO Steve Ballmer stopped doing Think Weeks. One young CEO, however, is reportedly interested in pursuing the habit: Mark Zuckerberg of Facebook. Given his youth, his ambition, and that he may overtake Gates as the richest individual in America, there would be a nice symmetry to it. —V.H.

FOR EVERY JACK WELCH, maybe there's a Bill Gates. If Welch used General Electric's sprawling teaching facility at Crotonville to continually reinvent the company (see Chapter 7), Gates at Microsoft did it all by himself. From 1992 to 2008, Gates' once- or twice-a-year Think Week was a Crotonville unto itself. Armed only with stacks of proposals and, later on, e-mails, Gates—sequestered from staff and family—recalibrated his company's strategic direction during his Think Weeks in the Pacific Northwest. It is where he thought of *The Road Ahead*, his first book; it was where the concept of Xbox Live got the green light; it is where the notorious "Internet Tidal Wave" memo began. Most companies are collegial. So was Microsoft. Its most significant products were born of teamwork. But the company's core always was singularly managed by Gates—and it was the odd, brilliant conception of Think Week that allowed him to contemplate, cogitate, and plot Microsoft's future.

Gates had spent idyllic childhood summers along the evergreen-lined shores of Hood Canal, southwest of Seattle. It made complete sense to him that he would retreat to the rustic family compound to do his Thoreau-cum-Adam-Smith thinking. Here, in an upstairs study with a portrait of Victor Hugo on the wall, was where he was most comfortable and could concentrate without distraction on the biggest picture. "I really wanted to be alone, just reading," he told me in an hourlong look back in the spring of 2012. "I don't eat breakfast, so the kitchen staff would bring me a lunch and a dinner. The chefs were very good, so in no sense was I deprived. That was my human contact during Think Week, except talking to my wife on the phone after I was married. That was my sole human contact." (When his wife,

Melinda, was pregnant one year, Gates did a Think Week at a hotel closer to Seattle, in case he had to rush back.) Diet Orange Crush sustained him during marathon 18-hour stretches. He kept a small refrigerator in the study so that he didn't have to waste time making the journey downstairs to the kitchen. If he needed a break, he might play bridge online.

Gates is thought of—fairly—as a ruthless businessman—driven by data, intolerant of incompetence, competitive to a fault. Yet there's another aspect to his psyche that prizes knowledge. In addition to chairman Gates, he can be professor Gates, knowing that he didn't know what he didn't know—and then attempting to master a field, be it world health policy or education reform at the Gates Foundation these days, or PC operating systems and antitrust defenses back when he was running Microsoft day to day. Think Week offered him the opportunity to immerse himself. We all have stacks of memos, articles, manuscripts, that haunt our offices and studies—the Perilous Piles or Towers of Doom. Think Week was Gates' way of taking them on, in a way that an occasional product-brainstorming session never could do.

"If you're an executive in a business where there's a lot of invention going on in universities, in small companies—and you have wild thinkers inside your own company—you want to have an hour to read a 15-page thing they wrote and then step back and think about it, give some feedback," Gates explained. "It's not easy when you have a fast and booming company—you're hiring, you're going out and meeting with customers, you've got quarterly earnings to deal with. As knowledge builds out and new things emerge from smart people in your own company, as well as from outsiders, you want to be up to date." You couldn't do that at company headquarters. "During the six days of Think Week, I did nothing other than reading and sleeping and eating."

The notion for Think Week, which had its roots in Gates' visits to his grandmother at the canal in the 1980s, was his alone. "There are people who take retreats and go off to fish," he said. But his idea was to skip the fun and devote the time to work. "I wanted to force myself to read five or six related papers and then go take a walk and then write up my thoughts about ... when do cameras really come in, when do robots really come in, when does speech translation get to being good enough, how do the various form factors—like phones vs. tablets—relate to each other?"

Initially, when Microsoft was in its youth, Gates read a lot of Ph.D. theses and scholarly papers from around the country. The academic material was typically suggested by Microsofties, based on something they'd heard. He also had various pieces of software demonstrated for him by Microsoft programmers, though that part of Think Week was separated out a few years later and became quarterly demo days at the company.

In time, most submissions to Gates were based entirely on internal projects and ruminations—often from lower-level researchers who had no managerial responsibility and whom Gates was unlikely to see even at a demo day. In that way, anyone at Microsoft—even as it grew to tens of thousands of employees—had a shot at gaining the boss's ear, and the boss was able to tap the wattage of his estimably able workforce. People knew that Gates really did deep dives into the material (and used clichés like "deep dive"), and the company, while not always the creator of elegant software, nonetheless aimed high. In one *Wall*

Street Journal article, a Microsoft manager described Think Week as "the world's coolest suggestion box." If the boss blessed a suggestion or okayed a proposal, it might be the biggest moment in your career. Though ideas were key for Gates, he well understood "the positive morale effect" that Think Week could have on employees.

Early on, according to Gates, he got about 50 submissions—on paper and brought to Hood Canal in cardboard boxes, with submissions color-coded by topic and stamped MICROSOFT CONFIDENTIAL. "I read them all and commented on them all," he said. "It was just me sitting there with a pen, and I would scribble on the thing and then go type up a Word document." Comments would go not only to the person who submitted a paper, but to a range of executives and engineers whom Gates thought should read them. Ultimately all his comments were put online on a SharePoint site, where they were categorized by topic. "I could then tell who read them and how long the comments were," Gates said. "And when I wanted to reply, I could just sit there electronically and type in my comments on various sections." Eventually all the submissions came in digital form.

That "very good infrastructure" proved essential as more Softies sent in material. By the mid-1990s Gates used an assistant to filter the submissions. It was always somebody who had a technical background and who, as Gates put it, "could read a lot of stuff and judge which things were going to be worth having me read or not read." The high-ranked items—they were actually ranked—first totaled about 120. During the last Think Weeks (they ended in 2008), the number had grown to nearly 400, so Gates' assistant had to create two categories: the submissions that Gates still read personally and those that wound up before another Microsoft executive. Normally Gates did not want a smorgasbord of topics. Instead, he preferred to drill down on a few areas. For example, when he was interested in visual recognition, he'd want to read all submissions on it. "I'd really be wanting to think, Okay, how big a bet should the company make on visual recognition? Or how does storage change when you get really cheap memory? How does that change the architecture of the database? Is Microsoft going to be out front on that?"

Most of what Gates saw Gates wasn't interested in. He said his comments largely were telling folks, "This stuff doesn't look very promising—let's not work on it." Some papers gave Gates overviews about coming consumer trends, like digital photography, interactive TV, the rise of wireless technology, and the ubiquity of GPS-enabled devices. Other papers brought him up to speed on ongoing technical concerns, like microprocessor improvements or Internet security or software piracy or— "one of my favorites!" he says—"everything related to semiconductors." Others were just flights of fancy—about, say, "magic mirrors" (which had something to do with letting you try on virtual outfits or informing you that your collar wasn't buttoned).

But now and then Think Week also gave Gates the time and space to reposition the corporate supertanker that Microsoft had become. His seminal "Internet Tidal Wave" memo of May 26, 1995, to Microsoft executives is the best illustration of what Think Week could spark. The memo was inspired by various material that employees had sent him. Still, it was Gates who saw the big picture—"the opportunity challenge," in his geekspeak—even if he was admittedly late to the challenge. In the memo, Gates recognized the threat and the hope of the Net, which he declared "the most important single development to come along since the IBM PC was introduced in 1981." So from that moment, he "assigned" the Net "the highest level of importance" to Microsoft. Most tellingly, he signaled his determination to "match or beat" the services provided by a Silicon Valley startup called Netscape, "a competitor 'born' on the Internet" that had a 70% share of the browser market. Thus began the browser wars, which led to the squashing of Netscape's web browser—and *U.S. v. Microsoft*, the Justice Department's antitrust suit against the company that was eventually settled in 2001.

Musing about the Tidal Wave memo made Gates think about Microsoft's being late to the party in other recent battles over Internet technology. He told me that "part of the fun of being in the technology business is being up-to-date," and "you don't want to feel like you're getting behind." So it was "really painful," he said, when a "trend got fairly well established before you know it's going on." Think Weeks were an effort to be ahead or at least not far behind. But Think Weeks could only be about identifying ideas. You still had to execute them, and Gates acknowledged that Microsoft, for example—notwithstanding discussions about Internet search—"didn't execute as well as Google did." Though "we were talking about it," he said, "the talent we put on it and the way we conceptualized it" weren't sufficient in retrospect. "That's always going to happen because there are thousands of companies trying specific things, and, you know, 999 of them fail. But there'll be one that has picked a very dedicated approach that does really catch on, and of course Google's the best example of that."

Some Think Week ideas have yet to be developed. Gates cites "how you organize memories of your kids in a digital world so you have an easy way to go back and look and find things—not just photos, but report cards, movies, comments, e-mails, and stuff."

Given Gates' success with Think Weeks, the wonder is they didn't continue after he left his day-to-day job at Microsoft in 2008. Or that other companies didn't try to imitate them. But Gates isn't particularly surprised by either. "People have different styles," he said. "Being able to comment on 120 papers and take six days where you're just totally focused on that, that's more my style than others' style…. I just kind of like that, you know, pushing myself super-hard." He's also a realist, knowing that if he alternatively had saved various papers e-mailed to him and had said to himself he would get to them someday, he never would have. Most CEOs or other leaders, he suggested, would behave the same way.

Gates has been asked about Think Weeks by several CEOs (whom he didn't wish to name) in such fast-changing industries as high tech, cars, drugs, and chemicals—but he had the sense that the practice was too "hard core" for them. He also said he thought some companies were too broad-gauged for a CEO to have Think Weeks.

Take General Electric. "It's kind of the extreme case," he said. "What are you going to get—a paper about polyethylene plastics, a paper about turbofan jet engines, a paper about mortgage derivatives coming out of GE Financial? It's so broad." What the CEO of GE is mostly doing is "picking people and business models. He's not really part of the question 'Are our refrigerators a breakthrough or not?'"

Even at Microsoft itself, the Think Week tradition ended. "There was a notion they might continue as a community exercise, even though people might not take a full week," Gates said. "But once I wasn't there, sort of as a key audience to write all these papers for—knowing there was a reasonable chance that I'd read them and write a thoughtful comment on them—then it didn't continue."

At his foundation, Gates doesn't do Think Weeks anymore. He said there's no reason to, since he no longer has an all-consuming managerial job. "I have more ability now to spend unstructured time" with top scientists, academics, doctors, and educators. And he goes to "invention sessions" at Intellectual Ventures (IV), a private investment and invention laboratory for fields ranging from software to biotechnology. IV was started by Nathan Myhrvold, the polymathic former chief technology officer for Microsoft. Gates uses his sessions at IV for topics on global health and says they can end up functioning like a Think Week on, say, malaria. "Because I'll get maybe 800 pages of material, more sometimes. I'll have to set aside 2½ days to read all that stuff to be ready," Gates said. In that sense, for Gates, the model of Think Weeks lives on.

9

SOFTSOAP'S BLOCKING DECISION

By **BRIAN O'KEEFE**

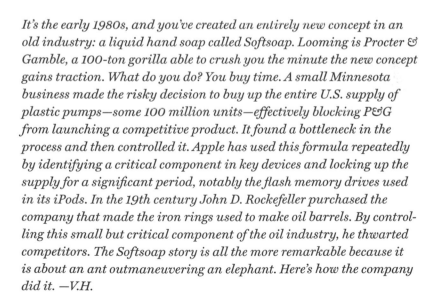

It's the early 1980s, and you've created an entirely new concept in an old industry: a liquid hand soap called Softsoap. Looming is Procter & Gamble, a 100-ton gorilla able to crush you the minute the new concept gains traction. What do you do? You buy time. A small Minnesota business made the risky decision to buy up the entire U.S. supply of plastic pumps—some 100 million units—effectively blocking P&G from launching a competitive product. It found a bottleneck in the process and then controlled it. Apple has used this formula repeatedly by identifying a critical component in key devices and locking up the supply for a significant period, notably the flash memory drives used in its iPods. In the 19th century John D. Rockefeller purchased the company that made the iron rings used to make oil barrels. By controlling this small but critical component of the oil industry, he thwarted competitors. The Softsoap story is all the more remarkable because it is about an ant outmaneuvering an elephant. Here's how the company did it. —V.H.

ROBERT TAYLOR knew he needed to do something radical. The inventive entrepreneur had just introduced a brilliant concept—hand soap in a pump bottle—that was roiling a centuries-old industry. Sales of his Softsoap were accelerating beyond his most optimistic projections. But experience had taught Taylor that his upstart company's success might be short-lived once soap-making giants like Procter & Gamble, Armour-Dial, and Colgate-Palmolive came to market with competing products. How could he slow down his larger rivals enough for his brand to gain lasting traction with customers?

The plan Taylor hatched was both elegantly simple and spectacularly bold. Like John D. Rockefeller before him, Taylor found a bottleneck in the system and owned it. More recently Apple has followed the same formula repeatedly—identifying a critical component in a key device, such as the flash memory drive used in its iPods, and locking up supply.

But Taylor's success with Softsoap was particular striking given the odds against him. "To get to market with something that's truly different is never easy, particularly when there are big incumbents that could choose to imitate you," says Hugh Courtney, dean of the College of Business Administration at Northeastern University and author of *20/20 Foresight: Crafting Strategy in an Uncertain World*. Taylor's success with Softsoap shows a high degree of what Courtney calls "allocentrism," or the ability to understand others and their propensity for action. That instinct gave Taylor the leverage to turn the tables on his rivals.

The story begins on a morning in 1977, when inspiration struck Taylor as he was driving to work. At age 41, he had already proved himself to be an unusually creative and ambitious businessman. After getting his Stanford MBA and working for two years in sales for Johnson & Johnson, Taylor had founded his own company, the Minnetonka Corp., in 1964 with $3,000 and a hunch that he could make money selling fancy, packaged gift soap. He set up shop in Chaska, Minn., just outside Minneapolis, and in the beginning he hired women to make hand-rolled soap out of their homes. Before long he had developed a network to distribute his Village Bath line of products to department stores and gift shops around the country.

Taylor was a font of ideas. He quickly expanded into body lotion, scented candles, bubble bath, and other items. In a single spring he once introduced 78 new products. Taylor took the company public in 1968, and by the late 1970s Minnetonka was up to $25 million in annual sales. He had added distributors in Europe, Canada, and Australia. But the restless CEO was casting about for a mass-market product that could take his company to the next level. He had already experienced a major setback when Clairol and Gillette knocked off his promising line of fruit-scented shampoo, rushed their own products to market, and squeezed him out.

As he steered his car through traffic that morning, Taylor kept picturing a sloppy bar of hand soap sitting on an otherwise pristine kitchen vanity—and how the ugly soap ruined the picture. "I thought, Well, why not put it in a beautiful container and have a pump and it's disposable?" says Taylor. "And it might be something that would appeal to housewives. So that's how that all started." He told his chemists to get to work, and they quickly developed a liquid soap that included emollients in a shampoo type of formula.

A few months later he introduced the Incredible Soap Machine. It was a pump-operated 16-ounce bottle of liquid soap with flowers on it that sold for $4.95 and came in a gift box. Taylor sold it in department stores, where it was a tremendous success. Women wrote letters to Minnetonka raving about the Soap Machine. But why, they wondered, couldn't they buy it in drugstores and convenience stores like regular bar soap? Spurred by the response, Taylor decided that if he reduced the size of the package, took the bottle out of the box, lowered the price, and gave it a more generic name, he might have a mass-market hit—if he could also get the right distribution and fend off the big boys.

In the late 1970s, according to a 1995 Harvard Business School case study by Adam Brandenburger and Vijay Krishna, the market for bar soap in the U.S. was about $1.5 billion in annual sales and was dominated by a handful of large companies. The dominant brands were Dial from Armour-Dial, followed by Ivory and Zest from Procter & Gamble. Lever Brothers, the U.S. subsidiary of Unilever and the maker of Dove, and Colgate-Palmolive, with Irish Spring, were right behind. The average price of a bar of soap was 23 cents. Innovation was in short supply.

By late 1979, Taylor was ready to launch his new mass-market liquid soap and had settled on a name: Softsoap. After months of test marketing, he had decided to sell it for $1.59 in a 10.5-ounce bottle, the equivalent of more than five bars of soap. Taylor went out and appointed 91 food brokers around the country to take Softsoap into territory that Minnetonka had never before penetrated: grocery and drugstores. The only problem was that many store managers wanted to put Softsoap in the health and beauty section; Taylor fought to get it placed right next to the bar soap so that customers would understand that it was an alternative to sloppy, traditional soap.

The response from test markets was so promising that early in 1980 Taylor took a huge gamble: He cut his first television ad and spent $7 million on a national campaign to introduce Softsoap. At first nothing happened. The company didn't get one reorder for three months. Inventory kept piling up. "My CFO came in to see me one day and said, 'Bob, have you got any more good ideas? Because this one just isn't moving through,'" says Taylor. But Taylor wasn't worried. He reminded the CFO that their research had shown that housewives, the target customers, needed to see a product at least three times on TV before it fully registered with them. Taylor was confident that a wave of sales would soon kick in. "Two weeks later we were out of stock on everything we had in the warehouse," says Taylor. "It was completely sold out, and then we chased demand for eight or nine months before we were ever able to catch up." By the end of the year Softsoap had brought in $39 million in sales.

At that point Taylor faced his biggest hurdle yet: competition. Dozens of imitation products hit the market from small competitors. Much more threatening was the fact that the big soap makers like P&G, Unilever, and Colgate were beginning to test products. To Taylor it was starting to look a lot like his experience with fruit-scented shampoo. "We felt the competition coming, and they were trying to cost us right out of the business," says Taylor. "They were selling liquid soap at their manufactured cost." He adds, "The only thing that I could think of was to slow them down."

At the beginning of 1981, Taylor phoned Calmar, the California company that manufactured all the plastic pumps for Softsoap, and asked the president and the sales manager to fly out for a major strategy session. When they arrived, Taylor told them that Minnetonka might want to buy as many as 100 million pumps that year. "Well, they almost jumped out of their seats because they had never taken an order that big in their lives," says Taylor. "I said, 'How would this affect your manufacturing?' And they said, 'It would pretty much close us down. We wouldn't be able to shift any production over to our other customers.'"

Committing to such a gargantuan order felt risky. The biggest order he'd ever placed before that was for about 5 million units. But Taylor was pretty sure he could swing it financially. "We had so much money flowing, we were filthy rich because of demand," he says. And he knew that it would be an effective way to temporarily cripple his competition. There was only one other manufacturer in the U.S. making plastic pumps at the time, and it didn't make the right kind to work in a mass-market product. China wasn't yet a factor in making the kind of product that required plastic-injection molding. It would take weeks and weeks for another manufacturer just to design and cut the steel for a pump mold. Taylor negotiated a price reduction with the Calmar executives and placed the order for 100 million pumps on the spot.

Taylor's gamble paid off big-time. His big competitors were stymied. "We had them by the short hairs," he says. "For a good year it delayed them." Sales of Softsoap continued to accelerate, and Minnetonka kept its No. 1 position in the growing market for liquid soap. Over the next few years Taylor developed Softsoap spinoffs for shower soap, work soap, and medical soap.

The large soap makers eventually did get to market and began to undercut Minnetonka on price. In 1983, P&G's Ivory brand liquid soap overtook Softsoap for the No. 1 spot in market share, according to the Harvard case study. Minnetonka lost money in both 1982 and 1983, and Taylor was forced to slash his workforce. But the established brand power of Softsoap gave Taylor time to retrench. He decreased the size of the Softsoap bottle to 7.5 ounces and lowered the price. By 1985, Softsoap was back as the No. 1 brand, with 36% of sales, in the over $100 million market for liquid soap.

Ever the innovator, Taylor expanded into markets beyond soap. In 1983, Minnetonka introduced Check-Up, the first antiplaque toothpaste in the U.S. and the first to be sold in a pump. But his larger rivals quickly rushed out their own pump and antiplaque products in the established brands, causing Check-Up's market share to wither.

Taylor found more success with fragrances. In 1980 he had bought the Calvin Klein Cosmetics business, and it began to take off in 1985 when he launched the perfume Obsession with a massive $17 million advertising campaign. It was a huge hit, with sales of $50 million in the first year. Then he brought out another wildly successful fragrance called Eternity. Taylor found the profit margins in the scent business to be much sweeter than in soap. "I could see that the consumer goods business was going to be a dogfight long term," he says. "I thought, I can take the same amount of capital and put it into Calvin Klein and make so much more money."

So when Colgate-Palmolive CEO Reuben Mark called Taylor

in 1987 to discuss buying Softsoap, he was ready to make a deal. He ended up selling the business to Colgate for $75 million. And then, a couple of years later, he sold the rest of the company to a subsidiary of Unilever, another of his old soap competitors, for $376.5 million. In the end the industry giants retained control of their markets, but not before Robert Taylor taught them a lesson in business strategy.

10

TOYOTA PURSUES ZERO DEFECTS

By **ALEX TAYLOR III**

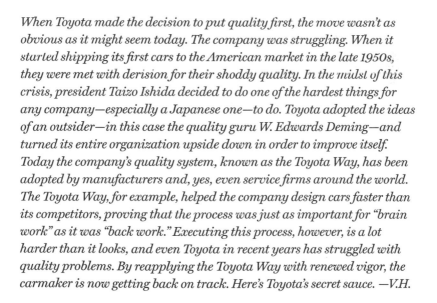

When Toyota made the decision to put quality first, the move wasn't as obvious as it might seem today. The company was struggling. When it started shipping its first cars to the American market in the late 1950s, they were met with derision for their shoddy quality. In the midst of this crisis, president Taizo Ishida decided to do one of the hardest things for any company—especially a Japanese one—to do. Toyota adopted the ideas of an outsider—in this case the quality guru W. Edwards Deming—and turned its entire organization upside down in order to improve itself. Today the company's quality system, known as the Toyota Way, has been adopted by manufacturers and, yes, even service firms around the world. The Toyota Way, for example, helped the company design cars faster than its competitors, proving that the process was just as important for "brain work" as it was "back work." Executing this process, however, is a lot harder than it looks, and even Toyota in recent years has struggled with quality problems. By reapplying the Toyota Way with renewed vigor, the carmaker is now getting back on track. Here's Toyota's secret sauce. —V.H.

IN 1961, TOYOTA STOPPED SELLING CARS in America and withdrew from the market in disgrace. It closed its offices in Chicago and San Francisco and moved its headquarters from Beverly Hills into rented space in Hollywood. The company had totally misread the U.S. market by trying to sell an underpowered, overpriced minicar with the durability of Kleenex. The company would not return to the U.S. until 1965, but when it did, it brought with it a new car with much higher quality at a more competitive price. That initiative launched a string of successes that now stretches over five decades. The story of how Toyota tried, failed, and then decided to try again in the American market—this with the help of an Iowa-born statistician named W. Edwards Deming—is unique in the annals of management.

Toyota got its start in 1925 as a maker of automatic looms and entered the car business in 1936. After the war, one of its early successes was the Toyopet, which, despite its tiny, 58-horsepower engine, had become popular with Japanese taxi drivers because of its ruggedness and reliability. An expansion-minded Toyota had already launched an export business by selling trucks in South America. Executives believed it made sense to combine the company's strengths and export cars as well. For that, they decided to target the world's single largest pool of customers: Americans.

The decision to target the U.S. came about this way, according to Toyota Jidosha Kabushiki Kaisha in *Toyota: A History of the First 50 Years*. Shotaro Kamiya, president of Toyota Motor Sales, had visited America on a business trip in 1955 and was astonished by the number of small cars he saw. Nearly 100,000 were on the road—all of them European and most of them Volkswagens. Toyota had been successful selling its Land Cruiser SUV overseas, so perhaps it could do the same with passenger cars. But Toyota would have to move quickly. Kamiya feared that the success of the Europeans would cause the U.S. to impose import restrictions. If the Japanese didn't establish a presence in the U.S., they risked being shut out.

Kamiya's proposal sparked a great debate within Toyota. Going up against GM, Ford, and Chrysler in their home market with small cars seemed too great a challenge for a company that had been making cars for such a short time. But Kamiya found a strong supporter in Taizo Ishida, president of Toyota Motor Corp. (The sales and manufacturing arms of Toyota operated as independent companies from 1950 to 1982.) Ishida had also visited the U.S. and noticed how little attention Detroit was paying to small cars. It was the era of V-8 engines and tailfins. Small cars like the Corvair and the Pinto wouldn't be introduced for another several years. Ishida had enjoyed success exporting Toyota's automatic looms overseas, and he believed that the company could do the same with passenger cars.

His arguments won the day. With minimum preparation, Toyota Motor Sales U.S.A. was incorporated in California in October 1957. It made its headquarters in Beverly Hills and found an old American Motors outlet in Hollywood to serve as its first dealership. On the showroom floor were the only Toyotas in the U.S: a pair of Toyopet sedans.

Toyota sold its first car early in 1958, and by year's end it had sold just 268 more, along with one Land Cruiser. The feeble sales performance was a sign of a larger problem: The Toyopet (later renamed the Crown) was not ready for primetime. In the rush to move into the U.S., Toyota had shipped an inferior product. It cost $700 more than a VW Beetle and wasn't nearly as good. The car vibrated badly at speeds over 60 miles an hour and tended to overheat when driven up mountains or in the desert. It also guzzled gas and stalled without warning.

Toyota had discovered that it was uncompetitive, but it was too late. In December 1960, just three years after it arrived and its reputation in tatters, Toyota suspended U.S. operations. It had sold fewer than 2,000 cars. For a proud company, it was a shameful moment.

Then Toyota made a decision that would not only reverse its fortunes but also would help revolutionize the way companies manufactured their products. It reached outside its own culture and adopted the quality ideas of an American business consultant. W. Edwards Deming, the father of total quality management, was about as charismatic as a metal-turning lathe. A formal man with rural roots, he dressed in worn three-piece suits and delivered lectures in blunt language. Unlike most consultants, who sell while they teach, he made little effort to win over his audiences; instead he confronted them with their own mistakes. The *New York Times* wrote that Deming "spoke to senior executives as if they were schoolboys." Yet Deming somehow managed to navigate that most complex of cultures, Japan's, and delivered a message that resonated with businessmen unused to being lectured by a *gaijin*. The Deming Prize, founded in his honor in 1950, immediately became highly sought-after by companies doing business in Japan, none more so than Toyota.

Trained as a mathematician, Deming had joined the U.S. Census Bureau and started to advise it on sampling techniques for the

1940 census. Deming left the Census Bureau in 1946 to begin a consulting practice, but a year later he was called to Japan by Gen. Douglas MacArthur's occupation government to advise on sampling techniques for a census aimed at quantifying the housing shortage in the nation. Deming spent his free time touring the country and made friends with several Japanese statisticians.

When his job was finished he moved back to America, becoming a professor at New York University. Deming returned to Japan in 1950 with an invitation from the Japanese Union of Scientists and Engineers to raise the level of the country's production standards. In June, Deming delivered the first of a dozen lectures to a standing-room-only crowd of 500. For the next three months he taught hundreds of engineers, managers, and scholars—and at least one group of top executives—statistical process control and quality improvement. Deming told the Japanese managers that if they followed his recommendations, "They would capture markets the world over within five years." His reassuring words to a country struggling to rebuild made him a hero.

Deming preached a simple doctrine as true today as when he first formulated it more than 80 years ago: Better quality will reduce expenses while increasing productivity and market share. He taught companies to treat production as a system, involving suppliers and consumers as well as the factory. In Deming's world, mass-produced items that were supposed to be identical always varied from one another in practice. Therefore, industrial processes should include a cycle for observing those variations and changing the process to reduce them. The defects should be analyzed, changes made, and the process refined until it was done right. His favorite saying was "In God we trust; all others must bring data."

His message particularly resonated with the post–World War II Japanese. Deming believed that top management was responsible for 85% of all defects and stressed the need for an appreciation of the individual worker. "The worker is not the problem," he said. "The problem is at the top." In *W. Edwards Deming: The Story of a Truly Remarkable Person*, Japan specialist Robert B. Austenfeld Jr. writes that Deming showed the Japanese respect at a time when their self-esteem was very low and the label MADE IN JAPAN was synonymous with shoddy, disposable goods. Deming's ideas dovetailed with many of Japan's own traditions. Japan had long held hard work and quality craftsmanship as important virtues. Deming preached that companies must treat workers as associates, not hired hands. "Break down barriers" and "drive out fear" were two of his guiding principles.

In 1961, still wounded by the failure of its U.S. initiative, Toyota decided to revamp its manufacturing system and adopt the Deming principles as part of a system of total quality control. Apparently it did so on its own initiative. There is no evidence that Deming ever visited the company or made any overtures, but it is clear that some at the company were familiar with his work. Now firmly committed to the passenger-car business, Toyota was making a determined effort to improve its processes in a fundamental way and achieve international levels of quality and cost. As a first step, it aimed to reduce processing defects, customer claims, and rework by 50%. It stated its goal publicly: It wanted to win the Deming Prize for quality control.

What Toyota discovered was that the dominant cause of product defects was wear in the machines that made the parts. As machines wore down, they produced defective parts; productivity suffered while workers waited for the machines to be fixed or replaced. So Toyota changed the way it operated its factories. First, it stopped moving workers around and assigned them responsibility for individual machines. Then it tackled dirt. Since dirt was responsible for the wear that was causing defects, workers were taught how to eliminate it. The last step in the equation was systematic preventive maintenance and immediate attention to problems. If a machine started vibrating, for instance, the operator was told to stop quickly and fix it. Years later Shoichiro Toyoda, now Toyota's honorary chairman, would explain, "We simply put quality first and follow through with the honest practice of developing quality products and quality people." He makes it sound simple, but the impact was revolutionary.

The Deming principles worked, and the message stuck. Four years after it had begun to apply the Deming principles, Toyota launched a sedan called the Corona that was specially engineered for American drivers. It was even more affordable than the Toyopet but featured luxuries like air conditioning, an automatic transmission, carpeting, sun visors, armrests, tinted windows, and a glove compartment. Moreover, it was designed to be internationally competitive and withstand the rigors of high-speed highway driving. During development, technical improvements were made to improve durability and handling. And the quality was vastly improved. Toyota went back to the U.S., and this time it was successful: The Corona sold well. It achieved another goal as well. In 1965, Deming returned to Japan to present the Deming Prize for major advances in quality improvement to Toyota's president, Fukio Nakagawa.

The success of Toyota would prove infectious. Eager to unlock its quality secrets, GM formed a joint venture to build cars with Toyota at an existing GM assembly plant in Fremont, Calif., beginning in 1984. GM's engineers expected Toyota's executives to be dazzled by the high technology and automated equipment at Fremont, but Toyota had it ripped out and replaced with older machinery. Miraculously, the same plant was producing 50% more cars, with fewer defects than before. Deming would have been amused. Years earlier he had observed, "American management thinks that they can just copy from Japan—but they don't know what to copy!"

Ford also tried to emulate Toyota. When Deming arrived at its Detroit headquarters in February 1981, Ford executives were expecting a slick presentation on quality. Deming, instead, insisted on asking about the company's culture and management philosophy. He questioned the way its managers operated and said that management actions were responsible for most of the problems in developing better cars. Statistical-control charts started appearing in the company's factories, and Ford adopted the slogan "Quality is job one." Ford CEO Don Petersen said, "We are moving toward building a quality culture at Ford, and the many changes that have been taking place here have their roots directly in Dr. Deming's teachings." Yet the lessons from Deming were forgotten when Ford became preoccupied with expansion. They weren't revived until 2006, when aerospace engineer Alan Mulally arrived from Boeing and brought Deming's principles with him. "My entire business approach is based upon Deming's continual quality improvement forever foundation,"

Mulally said. "It is really gaining momentum here at Ford again."

Unlike other quality consultants, Deming never built an organization around himself. As the *Times* pointed out in his obituary in 1993, he continued to work as a solo practitioner out of an office in the basement of his Washington, D.C., house. Aside from a brief spike in recognition from a 1980 NBC documentary, he remained mostly unknown to the general public, despite traveling widely on corporate assignments into his nineties. He never lost his characteristic bluntness. In the documentary he was asked, "If Japan can, why can't we?" Deming replied, "Anybody can produce quality if he lowers his production rate. That is not what I am talking about. Statistical thinking and statistical methods are to Japanese production workers, foremen, and all the way through the company a second language. In statistical control, you have a reproducible product hour after hour, day after day. And see how comforting that is to management—they now know what they can produce, they know what their costs are going to be."

Having mastered the second language of quality, Toyota never forgot it. It incorporated Deming's principles into the Toyota Production System, and it remains at the very top of the list of the automobile industry's highest-quality producers. Nor did it forget the lesson of what it meant to enter a market unprepared. The company is renowned for the amount of data it collects and the analysis it performs before making a big decision. When it gets things wrong—it needed three tries to develop a competitive minivan and is still trying to master the complexities of the American pickup-truck market—it simply reloads and tries again.

In the process of continuous improvement, Toyota grew to become the largest auto company in the world and, despite setbacks from natural disasters in 2011, it appears poised to regain its title. It never forgot the American who helped it get there. Accepting the American Society for Quality's Deming Medal in 2005, two years after its namesake's death, Toyoda offered this tribute: "He was an invaluable teacher ... playing an indispensable role in the development and revitalization of post-war Japan. As we continued to implement Dr. Deming's teachings, we were able to raise the level of quality of our products as well as enhance our operation at the corporate level. I believe that TMC [Toyota Motor Corp.] today is a result of our continued efforts to implement positive change in pursuit of the Deming Prize."

You could say, as they do in the Lexus commercials, that Toyota was committed to "the relentless pursuit of perfection."

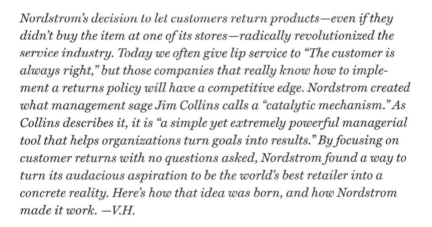

11

EXTREME CUSTOMER SERVICE

By **GEOFF COLVIN**

Nordstrom's decision to let customers return products—even if they didn't buy the item at one of its stores—radically revolutionized the service industry. Today we often give lip service to "The customer is always right," but those companies that really know how to implement a returns policy will have a competitive edge. Nordstrom created what management sage Jim Collins calls a "catalytic mechanism." As Collins describes it, it is "a simple yet extremely powerful managerial tool that helps organizations turn goals into results." By focusing on customer returns with no questions asked, Nordstrom found a way to turn its audacious aspiration to be the world's best retailer into a concrete reality. Here's how that idea was born, and how Nordstrom made it work. —V.H.

IT MUST BE SAID UP FRONT that the company says the tire story is absolutely true, though some people have wondered. What's much more important is that the story exists at all, and lives on. It's a powerful symbol, representing a business policy that has greatly benefited a large retailer, has influenced companies of all kinds around the world, and, believe it or not, holds the potential to nudge whole economies. (But more on the tire story later.)

All that's fairly impressive for a policy that began as a simple decision by three brothers running two shoe stores. We are talking about the return policy of Nordstrom, the Seattle-based retailer. The policy is that it will take virtually anything back and give you a refund, no questions asked, regardless of when the item was bought or whether you have a receipt. A beat-up five-year-old pair of shoes? Nordstrom will take them back. A jacket that you bought yesterday, wore to a party last night with the tags tucked inside, and are returning today? You'll get your money back, and you actually didn't have to leave the tags on. It's the most liberal return policy a retailer could adopt.

The decision wouldn't have seemed momentous back when it was made except that Nordstrom was then a small business in the Depression, and in those circumstances every decision is momentous. Everett, Elmer, and Lloyd were the sons of John Nordstrom, who had come over from Sweden at age 16. He tried his luck as a laborer and a potato farmer just outside Seattle, then made some money in the Klondike gold rush of 1897. When he returned to Seattle, he and another immigrant, Carl Wallin, started a little shoe shop (storefront: 20 feet) at Pike Street and Fourth Avenue. Wallin & Nordstrom kept moving to larger quarters and eventually opened a second store, but remained a small, local business.

John Nordstrom sold his interest to Everett and Elmer in 1928; Wallin sold them his interest (and removed his name) in 1929. Lloyd joined his brothers in 1933 after graduating from college. The three sons were now fully in charge of their two-store empire, just in time for the Depression's worst days.

Seattle went bankrupt. Hooverville shantytowns sprang up. Hardly anyone could afford new shoes. Nordstrom came within a month of shutting down. Somewhere in this period (even the brothers couldn't pinpoint exactly when), they made the ultimate contrarian move and adopted their super-liberal return policy. It would be satisfying to report that they foresaw the policy's extraordinary economic power, but that would not be accurate. The brothers just hated dealing with the obviously unjustified return claims that are a small but inevitable part of retailing, so they decided not to fight them. They told the clerks not to bother fighting them either. As Elmer explained (quoted in *The Nordstrom Way: The Insider Story of America's #1 Service Company* by Robert Spector and Patrick D. McCarthy), "We told them [the clerks], 'If the customer is not pleased, she can come to us and we'll give her what she wants anyway.'"

It follows that if a store will never dispute returns, then customers can return anything. Anything at all. Even, in theory, tires.

The tire story, if by some strange circumstance you've never heard it, is that a customer once returned a tire (or tires) to Nordstrom and got a cash refund—even though Nordstrom has never sold tires. The story has taken on the aura of myth, and Snopes.com, the website that investigates popular legends, has even concluded that it isn't true. But the company says it actually happened at the Fairbanks, Alaska, store in the 1970s. Nordstrom had recently moved into a building previously occupied by a business that did sell tires, and when a customer came in saying this was where he had bought his tires, the Nordstrom employees on duty decided to refund his money.

What matters is that the policy is real, and the story encapsulates it unforgettably. But it wouldn't be worth talking about if it were Nordstrom's only unusual trait. The return policy is the key element of an extreme customer service philosophy that has helped Nordstrom thrive and grow through an era when most regional retailers, as Nordstrom long was, failed or got bought by one of the national giants. Nordstrom created what management consultant Jim Collins calls a "catalytic mechanism." This is a galvanizing, non-bureaucratic way, as Collins puts it, to turn objectives into performance.

As with many of the best business decisions, the larger corporate environment makes it far more effective. Employees are given extraordinary latitude to make customers happy. On day one, new hires are also told Nordstrom's rules: "Rule No. 1: Use good judgment in all situations. There will be no additional rules." Thus, strictly speaking, Nordstrom has no spelled-out return policy. The de facto policy derives from empowered employees and a culture that guides them to move heaven and earth in finding a solution on behalf of the customer. One result is countless stories—true ones—about salespeople heroics. Running across the street to buy from a competitor (at a higher price) an item that Nordstrom didn't have in a customer's size. Sending a tailor to a dissatisfied customer's home to alter a suit—and then refunding the price of the suit, just because the customer was unhappy in the first place. Taking back shrunken shirts from a customer who admitted it was his fault—he hadn't followed the laundering instructions—and who wasn't even seeking a refund, just advice on how to undo the damage.

Such generosity may seem unwise to a hard-headed businessperson. But many research studies have shown that liberal return policies work—that they more than pay for themselves. The reasons are more numerous than you might suspect. They're revealed by the findings of behavioral economics, for which researchers have won Nobel Prizes. The Nordstrom brothers didn't win any Nobel Prizes, but they apparently understood human nature.

The most obvious effect of their policy is that it encourages people to buy; if you think you might be stuck with a purchase forever, you may refuse to purchase something even if you think—but aren't sure—you'd like it. Economists call this "regret avoidance." We are regret-minimizing machines. The pain of making a bad decision far outweighs the satisfaction of making a good decision on the same scale. Nordstrom's return policy takes regret out of the equation.

The policy also signals that Nordstrom merchandise is high quality. If it weren't, the company wouldn't be willing to guarantee it.

A subtler but surprisingly powerful element of the policy is what behavioral economists call the endowment effect. We value something that we own more highly than we value the same thing if we don't own it. That's irrational, of course, but a central finding of behavioral economics is that humans are fundamentally irrational. Ordinary items become treasured possessions once we own them, and the longer we own them, the more treasured they become.

The genius of the Nordstrom return policy is that it combines all those deep human tendencies. It makes the merchandise appear to be of high quality and makes buying things easy, since you know you can always return them—so if you can't decide between the blue suit and the gray suit, why not take them both home? There's no rush to choose once you get them home, since items are always returnable, so even if the blue suit isn't revving your engine, you may as well wait a bit longer, just to be sure. Yet after you've bought them, and the longer you own them, the endowment effect makes you ever less likely to return either one.

The business case for the no-questions-asked return policy is clearly strong. But anyone thinking of adopting a similar policy should be aware that it isn't as simple as it may seem. As effective as the policy has long been, it also gives rise to four paradoxes that Nordstrom has had to manage skillfully:

▶ Nordstrom isn't a charity. It's a ferociously competitive, growth-oriented retailer, and salespeople are expected to meet ambitious sales goals—meaning net sales, or sales minus returns. So sales staff are getting potentially conflicting signals: Move as much merchandise as possible out the door, but take back anything and everything with a smile.

▶ Nordstrom pays salespeople by commission, which at other retailers can lead to awful customer experiences with predatory, high-pressure clerks. A key element of Best Buy's success in the 1990s was the elimination of sales commissions, which improved the customer experience, while Circuit City continued to pay commissions; Circuit City finally eliminated commissions too, but too late, and it failed. Nordstrom wants its salespeople to be a customer's trusted adviser while also motivating them to sell each customer as much as possible.

▶ Nordstrom holds frequent internal sales competitions, pitting sales staff against one another. Motivating a salesperson to take sales away from a colleague, which is how such competitions play out at other retailers, seems a dicey strategy for achieving great customer service.

▶ The most fundamental paradox is that as the return policy has taken on a life of its own, it can appear to contradict the use-your-judgment policy of freedom and discretion for salespeople. The contradiction appears explicitly in a story from the Spector and McCarthy book. It reports that Bruce Nordstrom, CEO in the 1970s and 1980s, would tell salespeople, "If a customer came into the store with a pair of five-year-old shoes and complained that the shoes were worn out and wanted her money back, you have the right to use your best judgment to give my money away. As a matter of fact, I *order* you to give my money away." Yet ordering salespeople to do anything is not the Nordstrom way.

How has Nordstrom managed those paradoxes? The answer is the culture, the norms and values that pervade daily life in the company and that say we can balance the contradictions in those paradoxes; we know they'll all work out—we know the big-picture strategy works. That's a cautionary message for companies drawn to the no-questions-asked return policy but lacking the supporting culture, because culture change is never quick or painless.

A liberal return policy obviously costs money, and Nordstrom continues to believe that the cost is a good investment. But fraud and abuse of retail return policies appear to be getting worse. The National Retail Federation estimates that 8% of all returns in the U.S. are fraudulent, costing some $18 billion annually, and fraudulent returns are growing faster than retail spending. The problem goes far beyond shoppers who return clothes after one or two wearings (called "wardrobing" in retail) or who return non-defective merchandise that has simply worn out. Some people go dumpster diving to find receipts for items that were bought with cash; then they go to the store, shoplift those items, and take them to the return counter with the receipts. It's a brilliant scheme; a fence will pay only a fraction of a stolen item's price, but the return counter pays 100%. And at Nordstrom you don't even need the receipt.

It's unlikely that Nordstrom would ever change its stated policy, but like other retailers, it's using information technology to keep better track of customers and their behavior. It can identify those who abuse the return policy, at least some of them, and in rare cases it will even ask a serial abuser not to come back.

Nordstrom is nearly unique in accepting returns at any time even without a receipt. (Other retailers—Kohl's, REI, L.L. Bean, Costco—also accept returns without a time limit but do require a valid receipt.) Because of its extraordinary customer service overall, Nordstrom has been America's most influential retailer by far, cited by consultants and business professors, reported on by *60 Minutes*, and studied by managers in many industries who want to serve customers better.

Could Nordstrom even influence a country? Chinese retailers generally don't permit returns, or do so only within severe limits. Chinese consumers are notoriously stingy shoppers; they spend little and save almost 40% of their incomes. Researchers at China's Renmin University asked consumers about factors that might influence their buying: income, interest rates, retailer credibility, shopping-environment comfort, the retail return policy, and others. The most important factor, consumers said, was the return policy. They estimated they would buy 27% more if offered a lenient return policy. They said they passed up buying opportunities a huge 43% of the time because of uncertainty.

China's top economic priority is growing its consumer economy—getting people to buy more. In the past, when the country focused on expanding its technology and industrial sectors, it learned from Western scientists and manufacturers. Maybe now it's time to learn something from a certain retailer.

12

TAKING THE STING OUT OF A PAINFUL SITUATION

By **GEOFF COLVIN**

Tata Steel faced a problem that has confronted many companies before and since: how to get rid of lots of people. Do it well, and your company becomes more competitive while your former employees go on to productive careers elsewhere and tell the world the company is a fair, honorable institution. Do it badly, and your productivity stagnates because the best people leave and you're reviled by media, politicians, and society for being heartless and greedy. Tata Steel's CEO made a decision that led to a novel downsizing approach that today's leaders should heed. One can't help but think it paid off in many different ways. Perhaps years later the Tata Group found it easier to win government and union approvals of its international deals, such as its acquisitions of Tetley Tea, Corus Steel, and Jaguar Rover Group. Here's how Tata did it. —V.H.

WHEN J.J. IRANI WALKED into his regular quarterly meeting with the shop stewards at the steel plant he managed, he knew this meeting would not be regular. He would be discussing very bad news, news that no one in the room had ever heard before. This was the sprawling, rusting, smoking, antiquated Tata Steel plant in the town that Tata Steel had built, Jamshedpur, India. The year was 1993. The news was that some employees were actually going to lose their jobs.

It was unbelievable. No one ever lost his job at Tata Steel. It existed to give people jobs. Once you worked there, your job was guaranteed, and after 25 years you were guaranteed that your son or daughter could also work there. It was beyond life-time employment; it was eternal employment.

Of course, it had to end, and now Irani had to explain why. As he began, one of the shop stewards stood up and shouted, "You're taking away our sons' jobs!" Irani responded, "You're worried about your son's job, but I'm worried about your job and my job. If we don't make these changes, neither one of us will have a job."

In retrospect, he says, that was a turning point in his campaign to convey the new reality: "The message was sent how very sick we were."

Tata Steel's basic problem of inefficiency wasn't unusual, but its severity was incredible. The company responded with an uncommon solution, one that in fact seemed crazy—irrational on its face. When an Indian industrialist heard about it, he sent Irani a note: "You either have too much money or not enough brains." Yet Irani's solution has proved to be one of the wisest decisions in the whole realm of employee relations and corporate culture.

For the 40 years before 1991 it hadn't mattered that Tata Steel was egregiously uncompetitive vis-à-vis the world's other big steelmakers. The country's closed, socialistic economy kept foreign competitors out, and domestic competitors, including Tata itself, were under tight government control. In India's through-the-looking-glass system, inefficiency was good and efficiency was bad. The main responsibility, dictated by the government, of a large company like Tata Steel was to employ lots of people—the more, the better. Costs weren't a worry; government controllers ensured that the company would sell what it made. Of course, the amount of steel the company made each year was set by the government. That's how efficiency became a sin; producing more than the specified output was illegal, and companies could be prosecuted for it.

In any case, there was no reason to buck the system. Irani explains, "The government told us what to make, how much to make, who to sell to, and how much to charge. What we paid in salaries was recompensed to us by the government through the steel price. If someone in the government asked for a job for a niece or nephew, Tata Steel would more often than not say okay." As a result, he says, "we had no incentive to modernize."

Everything changed in 1991, when India finally faced economic reality. The rest of the world had been booming through the 1980s, and the communist countries had finally thrown off their chains, but India was crumbling and starving. After a balance-of-payments crisis in early 1991, requiring an International Monetary Fund bailout, the government launched the radical changes of converting the economy from socialism to capitalism. That meant deregulation, privatization, and opening up to international trade. Tata Steel's incentives didn't just shift; they suddenly reversed.

Now competing against the world's best steelmakers, Tata Steel had to get radically better, and fast. Its facilities and processes were ancient. The company didn't know how many employees it had and needed three months to figure out the total (about 78,000). They included some 3,000 secretaries and office boys. The accounting department employed 32 chauffeurs, security people, and "peons," a job category that translates as "gofer" in American English. The company had a department that made paint and another that made ice. It had a dairy farm. Those were not features of a sleekly competitive modern steelmaker.

Tata Steel was producing about 100 tons of steel per man-year. An efficient producer like America's Chaparral Steel was producing about 1,000 tons per man-year. Yes, those Indian man-years were less expensive, but not enough so.

Tata Steel faced a problem that has confronted many companies before and since: how to get rid of lots of people. Do it well, and your company becomes more competitive while your former employees go on to productive careers elsewhere and tell the world the company is a fair, honorable institution. Do it badly, and your productivity stagnates because the best people leave, while you're reviled by the media, politicians, and society for being heartless and greedy. Solving the problem is never easy—but unique factors made it extraordinarily difficult for Tata Steel.

The challenges began with the vast Tata enterprise's unusual role in Indian society. The founding genius, Jamsetji Nusserwanji (J.N.) Tata, was an ardent nationalist who wanted India to be prosperous, peaceful, and free of British rule. He was also a follower of the Parsi religion, as his descendants, who have continued to run the company, remain to this day. The religion is founded on the notion that life must be dedicated to charity and justice. From the beginning of his career, J.N. Tata, who had studied to be a Parsi priest, was pursuing goals much larger than profit.

After starting the business as a trading house in 1868 and then getting rich manufacturing textiles, Tata formed a long-term plan of how his family would influence India's future. Besides continually expanding into new businesses, he established a charitable trust, the J.N. Tata Endowment for Higher Education, in 1892. Tata charities have since proliferated almost beyond number, into medicine, science, education, the arts, sports, and other fields; they have touched millions of Indians. Like all his successors, J.N. Tata left the bulk of his wealth to charitable foundations, so that today various trusts own about two-thirds of Tata Group. The company is fiercely competitive, but as a former managing director, Alan Rosling, has said, "We make money so our owners can give it away."

Tata Group also had established a long record of treating workers better than it had to and better than other employers did. It was among the first companies anywhere to adopt an eight-hour workday (in 1912), maternity benefits (1928), and profit sharing (1934).

A mass firing clashed loudly with Tata's heritage and with India's expectations of the company. Compounding the challenge was Tata Steel's location. Most of Tata Steel's operations were in the remote town of Jamshedpur—where iron ore, fuel, and water transport were all available—a town Tata Steel built and which J.N. Tata had begun planning before his death in 1904. It was and remains a company town in the best sense: Workers get free housing, free medical care, and free education, all of it high quality. Streets are wide and parks plentiful. The U.N. in 2004 included Jamshedpur among six global examples of excellent urban planning. The problem is that when Tata Steel fires workers in Jamshedpur, no other major employer exists to hire them. It's like throwing them overboard.

That was the environment in which J.J. Irani had to design a plan for firing thousands of workers. A labor union represented the workers, so Irani began by making his case to its leaders. The union hadn't called a strike since the 1920s, and both sides wanted to maintain peace if possible. But Irani was emphatic that a few things would have to change. The central fact was that huge numbers of workers had to go. In addition, the union would have to agree to eliminate the rule that guaranteed sons and daughters a job. "I told the union this cannot proceed," Irani recalls. "Otherwise we'd just have a one-for-one substitution and never get a reduction." Beyond the union's accepting that change, Irani didn't expect much help from it. "I told them I understand no union can recommend to its members a reduction in force," he says. So he didn't ask union leaders to endorse the action; he just asked them not to oppose it.

Irani took his time, partly to make sure employees understood the reasons for the change and partly so he could devise the right program. He didn't begin implementing the plan, called the Early Separation Scheme (ESS), until 1994. Here's how it worked.

The company chose the workers who would be offered the exit package—"otherwise the best people would have gone," says Irani. Those offered the package could decline it and keep their jobs, but if they later decided they wanted the package, it would be less generous.

And it was startlingly generous. Workers under age 40 would be guaranteed their full salary for the rest of their working lives, until normal retirement at age 61. Older workers would be guaranteed an amount greater than their salary, from 20% to 50% greater depending on their age. If they died before reaching retirement age, their families would keep receiving the full payments until the worker would have reached that age. If they continued to live in Jamshedpur, they and their dependents—sons younger than 21, unmarried daughters, and parents—would continue to get free medical care; if they left, they'd get free medical insurance. They would have to give up their company housing, but there was no rush; they'd have three years to find someplace else.

The ESS was so lavish that it raises an obvious question: If the objective is to become more efficient and reduce labor costs by getting rid of workers, then what could possibly be the point of giving those workers their full salaries—or more—plus benefits, for their entire working lives? Financially it would be as if they'd never left, yet they wouldn't be around to do any work. That's why the industrialist wrote Irani the letter about Tata having excess money or insufficient smarts.

That assessment turned out to be mistaken. The program wasn't as economically crazy as it first appeared. While workers who took the offer would get their full salaries or more, that amount would stay constant until age 61 instead of increasing, as it would if they remained employed; nor would Tata Steel have to pay payroll tax or make retirement plan contributions. Tata Steel's labor costs would begin to decline immediately, though gradually, and over time would decline more rapidly as recipients of the package reached retirement age in growing numbers. In the meantime, they could take another full-time job—Tata provided intensive counseling in how to get one— and earn far more in total than they would have made at Tata.

The ESS continued for years and is still used intermittently. By 2004, Tata Steel's workforce had shrunk from 78,000 to 47,000, with about a third of the reduction from natural attrition. Lower labor costs combined with over $1 billion of new investment turned Tata Steel into a far more efficient, globally competitive firm.

Companies around the world have gone through the same basic transition, but few have had to transform their culture so radically. Tata Steel's mission for decades had been to create jobs, not wealth, to employ bureaucrats' nephews and then their sons and grandsons. Now its stance had to change dramatically—"from patriarchal to practical," as the company later put it—without wrecking Tata Group's elevated place in Indian society. The ESS achieved that goal and set the stage for 20 years of unprecedented excellent performance by Tata Group. Did it pay off in other ways, perhaps by easing government and union approvals of Tata Group's later international deals, such as its acquisitions of Tetley Tea, Corus Steel, and Jaguar Rover Group? There's no direct evidence that it did. But one can't help suspecting.

More broadly, this decision by an inefficient company in a failing Third World economy set an example that Western companies now find useful years later. Research shows that the public in the developed world distrusts business more than ever; people increasingly judge companies not by operating results but by how they treat employees and by their role in society. Tata understood those dynamics long ago. Turns out the company had plenty of brains. The money followed.

13

BOEING BETS BIG ON THE 707

By **ADAM LASHINSKY**

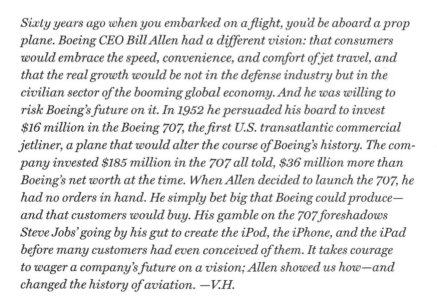

Sixty years ago when you embarked on a flight, you'd be aboard a prop plane. Boeing CEO Bill Allen had a different vision: that consumers would embrace the speed, convenience, and comfort of jet travel, and that the real growth would be not in the defense industry but in the civilian sector of the booming global economy. And he was willing to risk Boeing's future on it. In 1952 he persuaded his board to invest $16 million in the Boeing 707, the first U.S. transatlantic commercial jetliner, a plane that would alter the course of Boeing's history. The company invested $185 million in the 707 all told, $36 million more than Boeing's net worth at the time. When Allen decided to launch the 707, he had no orders in hand. He simply bet big that Boeing could produce— and that customers would buy. His gamble on the 707 foreshadows Steve Jobs' going by his gut to create the iPod, the iPhone, and the iPad before many customers had even conceived of them. It takes courage to wager a company's future on a vision; Allen showed us how—and changed the history of aviation. —V.H.

HERE'S A SHOCKER to even the casual student of aviation history under the age of, say, 75. At the dawn of the jet age Boeing, one of today's dominant makers of commercial aircraft, was a nonentity in the business of building planes for airlines. That's right. In the years following World War II, when U.S. industry was retooling for civilian production, Boeing was primarily a maker of military aircraft.

Its famous B-52 bomber and a companion tanker had proved that the Seattle company had the right stuff when it came to jet aircraft technology. But for the airlines, jets weren't commercially viable: Converting to jet technology would require a massive investment that could pockmark their bottom line. Instead, as late as the mid-1950s civilian fliers bounced along at relatively low altitudes in noisy, uncomfortable, slow-moving piston-engine aircraft like the Douglas DC 6, the Boeing 377 (also known as the Stratocruiser), and the Lockheed Constellation.

Yet Boeing, while well positioned to take advantage of the shift to superior jet engine technology, was ill equipped to make the case for airlines. By then the aeronautics giant had endured a 20-year string of financial flops—the Clipper, the Stratocruiser, and the Stratoliner. It seemed Boeing didn't have the right DNA when it came to selling to customers who weren't in uniform. It did count airlines as customers, but Boeing's salespeople weren't well respected, its track record was poor, and its engineers viewed warriors, not tourists, as their end users.

In the eyes of the airlines, Boeing competitor Douglas Aircraft was everything the Seattle company was not. With the exception of the war years, Douglas had been building commercial aircraft uninterrupted since 1934. The stalwart Douglas-built DC-3 had ruled commercial air corridors for years. Like a later era in the computing industry, when corporate buyers "never would be fired for buying from IBM," airline executives in the 1950s had the tightest of relationships with Douglas, whose planes were manufactured in Santa Monica. Few airline big shots even knew anyone at Boeing, whose bombers were built in Seattle. If any manufacturer was going to drag airlines along to the jet age party, the betting was on Douglas, not Boeing, playing host.

As if unfamiliarity with its customers weren't enough of an obstacle, Boeing faced another challenge as it pondered its move into passenger jets: safety. At the time, the flying public was spooked by a series of crashes of jets manufactured by Britain's De Havilland, whose Comet would later become the first commercial jetliner to fly a scheduled transatlantic route. With the Comet grounded in the mid-1950s, any decision to embrace jets would involve convincing passengers as much as the airlines themselves of the virtues of jet travel.

In other words, the safe choice for Boeing would have been to stick to its defense industry knitting. The U.S. Air Force—and other air forces around the world allied with America—would need Boeing's bombers and tankers in the expanding Cold War. Boeing could simply have stayed the course.

That wouldn't be the plan of Boeing's post-war president, William McPherson Allen. Boeing's culture was one where its workers enjoy doing big, adventurous things—like building some of the best, fastest, and most accurate bombers in the world. In that spirit, Allen made a prototypical great decision, an honest-to-goodness bet-the-company move on civil aviation in the form of a single product.

A graduate of Harvard Law School who had joined Boeing as its corporate counsel, Allen turned down an offer to become Boeing's president in 1944 because he thought an engineer should run the company. Once he'd been persuaded to take the job, however, Bill Allen provided the strategic leadership Boeing needed. He was convinced that consumers would cotton to the speed, convenience, and comfort of jet travel, and that the real growth would be in the civilian sector of the booming global economy, most importantly in the U.S. Allen was so sure of his conviction that he was willing to risk Boeing's financial future on it. In 1952 he persuaded the Boeing board of directors to invest $16 million in what would become the Boeing 707, the first U.S. transatlantic commercial jetliner and the plane that would alter the course of Boeing's history. It was just one plane, but it remade a company, an industry, and the very culture of its time.

There was nothing obvious in Allen's determination to push forward with the 707, and Boeing's deficiencies in the civilian-airline market were only part of the problem. "I think it's the biggest business decision of the 20th century," said Michael Lombardi, Boeing's corporate historian. "That decision just flipped the market around. There was no demand at the time for jet airplanes. The airlines weren't interested. And Boeing had a real opportunity to expand business with the Air Force." The demand issue was real. When Boeing's wide-bodied 747 made its debut more than a decade later, the company had an order in hand from Pan Am World Airways before production began. With the 707, Boeing's Allen simply bet that if company could produce it—then customers would buy it.

Allen used the $16 million the board had allocated to build

a prototype, known as the Dash-80. It built only one Dash-80, but the craft also served as a prototype for a jet tanker. It is at this point that Boeing received some generous and serendipitous aid from the U.S. government. The company secured an early order for a handful of jet tankers from the Air Force that helped justify the investment in the Dash-80. The deal also bought the aircraft maker the time it needed to get the airlines excited about a new passenger aircraft, loosely based on the Dash-80, that would be renamed the 707. (According to Lombardi, the company had always assigned sequential model numbers to its designs, and "700" was next up for its new line of jets. Marketing department executives decided that "Model 700" did not have a good ring to it, so they decided to skip ahead to Model 707, which seemed catchier.) The first production version of the 707 flew a test flight on Dec. 20, 1957, five years after the plane had been commissioned.

When the plane was ready to launch, Boeing encountered another stumbling block. Simultaneously Douglas had been developing a jetliner itself: the DC-8, which would have capabilities similar to the 707's. It was the beginning of a competitive trend in the aeronautics industry. Today Airbus typically develops similar aircraft at the same time Boeing rolls out a new model. Airlines unsurprisingly placed orders first with Douglas, whose model had the advantage of being an inch wider than the prototypes for the 707. In another big bet for an already expensive product, Boeing revamped its design, making the 707 an inch wider than the DC-8—which helped Boeing secure its first orders from Pan Am. So ill-prepared was the Boeing sales force that Allen assigned his own executives to call on airline accounts. United Airlines and then others followed suit after Pan Am, and the success of the 707 was assured. (The eleventh-hour retooling meant that the 707 never would become hugely profitable for Boeing. But the market share it gained enabled future planes to make up for the 707's financial shortcomings.)

The 707 was like nothing airline passengers had seen. The plane that became the long-range mainstay for Pan Am and other airlines—the 707-320—was 153 feet long, had a wingspan of 146 feet, and could fly 3,735 nautical miles. Getting airline executives to write the check to buy Boeing's planes was one thing. Persuading the flying public to get on board was something else. Boeing launched a print and broadcast advertising campaign that emphasized safety, comfort, and speed. The tagline for one memorable ad: "Only seven hours to brush up on your French." It was a visionary use of business-to-consumer advertising for a business-to-business product, a decision not unlike the one Intel made. (See Chapter 6.) Average consumers obviously do not buy airplanes any more than consumers choose a computer based on the chip inside (before Intel's famous campaign). They also don't typically choose an airline based on the make of aircraft the airline flies. Yet how many frequent fliers still think of the phrase, drilled into their heads by the aircraft maker's consumer campaign, "If it ain't Boeing, I ain't going." It also is a classic example of doubling down on a big bet by supporting an investment with additional investment.

Much as the U.S. was beaten to the punch in its space program by the Russians, a U.S. jet aircraft was not the first to ply the Atlantic commercially. British Overseas Airways Corp. flew first, from London to New York, on Oct. 4, 1958, with a

De Havilland Comet 4. But Pan Am was a fast follower—and ultimately a superior one. The maiden commercial flight of the 707 was on Oct. 26, 1958, three weeks after the BOAC flight. A first-class seat sold for $505. The back of the plane went for $272. (The prices were comparable to what customers would have paid on piston-engine planes.) Strong headwinds caused the Pan Am flight, dubbed the "Clipper America," to stop for refueling in Newfoundland. But when the plane touched down at Le Bourget Airport in Paris eight hours and 41 minutes after leaving New York, a new era in civil aviation was born.

The 707 grew to become as much a cultural icon as a transportation vehicle. The swimwear company Jantzen called its swimsuit line "the 707." Every U.S. president from Dwight D. Eisenhower to George H.W. Bush flew on an *Air Force One* that was a modified version of a 707. All told, Boeing invested $185 million in the 707. According to a 1957 article in *Fortune*, that was $36 million more than Boeing's net worth the previous year. The transformation for Boeing was complete. In later years its wide-bodied 747 would dominate long-haul and international travel. Its smaller 737 would become the workhorse of airlines around the world, a reliable, cost-efficient aircraft whose standard parts remain widely available. Boeing so thoroughly bested its erstwhile foe Douglas Aircraft that when Boeing bought McDonnell Douglas (the result of an earlier merger), it was primarily to boost its military offerings. In this way, Boeing returned to its roots, a reminder of where it had been before the 707 changed everything for the company—and transformed the history of aviation.

14

IBM'S OPERATION BEAR HUG

By **ADAM LASHINSKY**

In the early 1990s, IBM had hit a wall. It was hemorrhaging money as well as losing market share, a victim of the trend toward personal computers and away from IBM's mainframes. Lou Gerstner, who had been a McKinsey consultant and then CEO of American Express, was called in ostensibly to break up Big Blue. But first Gerstner made a decision to ensure that IBM's leadership was "back in touch" with reality. In what he called Operation Bear Hug, Gerstner and his lieutenants traveled the world talking to key customers. What they heard changed the destiny of the computer giant and eventually made it one of the most valuable companies in the world. Often senior management too quickly gets isolated from the realities of the market-place. Operation Bear Hug, a unique "first 100 days" initiative among Fortune 500 CEOs, was an antidote to that—and an approach more companies would do well to emulate. —V.H.

IN 1990, THREE YEARS BEFORE LOU GERSTNER was named chief executive of the beleaguered computing giant IBM, another iconic U.S. company ran a brilliant television ad. A balding CEO, suit jacket off but tie and vest on, addresses his assembled executives to let them know that their firm had been fired that morning by one of its oldest customers. "After 20 years, he fired us," says the executive. "He said he didn't know us anymore." The CEO then explains that the company had lost touch with its customers, that it relied too much on phone calls and faxes—this was 1990, remember—and not enough on face-to-face communication. Then (cue the solo piano tones of George Gershwin's "Rhapsody in Blue," which became a United Airlines anthem at the time), the executive's secretary begins handing out plane ticket envelopes with the familiar United logo on them. The CEO explains, "We're going to set out for a little face-to-face chat with every customer we have." When one of his executives objects, "But, Ben, that's got to be over 200 cities," our hero replies, "I don't care." Ben, of course, will visit that "old friend who fired us this morning." United's point is crystal clear in less than 60 seconds of airtime: Get back in touch with your customers—and fly our airplanes to do it.

Louis V. Gerstner required slightly longer than a minute to figure out that IBM, too, had a problem relating to its customers. But not much more. His decision to implement a real-life version of United's fictionalized CEO's directive was among the most important things he did upon joining IBM in 1993. That one decision—to embrace IBM customers in what became known as Operation Bear Hug—led to a cavalcade of other decisions. Taking what he learned from his customers, Gerstner in short order lowered prices on mainframe computers, sold off unproductive assets (including the company's prized art collection), and chose not to break up IBM (as everyone expected him to do). Most important, he emphasized and invested in a then insignificant part of IBM's business: consulting. Gerstner saw that it could help customers integrate the disparate pieces of technology they had purchased from IBM and others over the years.

In so many ways Gerstner was not the obvious choice to run IBM, for decades the world's preeminent technology company. After all, he was not a technologist. Originally a McKinsey management consultant, he had run credit card issuer American Express, essentially a marketing operation. He also had been the turnaround leader of cigarette and cookie maker RJR Nabisco, at the time the merged result of the largest and most controversial leveraged buyout of its day. The IBM he joined was losing money as well as market share, a victim of the trend toward personal computers and piecemeal software applications—both the opposite of IBM's mainframe computers with their integrated software. Its stock price had plummeted from $43 in 1987 to $12 in early 1993, when Gerstner met IBM stockholders for the first time.

Gerstner's hiring largely was greeted with derision. "Gerstner lacks any real knowledge of the computer industry, so he was apparently brought in to run IBM like a holding company of various businesses—more like a General Electric, with its range of divisions producing everything from light bulbs to jet engines, than like the completely integrated IBM of the past," wrote journalist Paul Carroll in his definitive 1993 account of IBM's demise, *Big Blues: The Unmaking of IBM*. Carroll, whose book went to press shortly after Gerstner joined IBM, asserted that Gerstner would "be able to apply only management-consulting dogma to IBM," as opposed to the grand vision or breakthrough products that had carried the company in earlier days. Without either of those, Carroll wrote, "Gerstner will just be fiddling."

Gerstner knew a few things well, however. For starters, he used a computer, unlike his predecessor at IBM, John Akers. (Still, in an early meeting with the news media, he couldn't identify the brand of laptop he used.) Critically, at American Express he was a large buyer of information technology. As such, he understood a common complaint he began hearing from IBM's customers: that the new era of individualized software programs and noncompatible equipment was causing headaches for corporate IT buyers. In other words, he understood the plight of the IBM customer because he had been one.

Indeed, weeks after joining IBM, Gerstner met with a group of top customers and explained his perspective. "I began by telling my audience that a customer was now running IBM," Gerstner wrote in his book, *Who Says Elephants Can't Dance?*, which he published in 2002. "I had been a customer of the information technology industry far longer than I would ever be an IBM employee, [and] while I was not a technologist, I was a true believer that information technology would transform every institution in the world."

Gerstner was appalled by the lack of customer orientation he found at the ultrapolitical and heavily bureaucratic IBM. He saw more infighting than he saw concern for the needs of customers. At the time IBM executives had assistants assigned to them who were up-and-coming executives themselves. They served a staff function and distinguished themselves by preparing detailed presentations rather than by having intimate knowledge of their customers. Customers polled by Gerstner early in his tenure were so dissatisfied that he told the same audience, "Everything at IBM would begin with listening to our customers and delivering the performance they expected."

The shocking state of affairs was in stark contrast to IBM's customer-focused legacy. Harvard management professor Bill George, who had previously run medical-device manufacturer Medtronic, had a summer job at IBM in the 1960s, when IBM was as powerful as a sovereign nation. Back then, IBM "was the business community's role model for customer service," George wrote in his book *Authentic Leadership: Rediscovering the Secrets to Creating Lasting Value.* He recounts an internal sales conference—which he compared to a religious rally—in which a senior official displayed a map showing each instance of a company that had bought products from an IBM competitor. "Our sales team was dispatched to visit 100% of these customers over the next two days and convert them to IBM—now!"

Gerstner claims not to have been a committed student of IBM's history. Yet he understood that listening to customers held the key to improving the fortunes of a company with a still powerful but diminishing market presence. In fact, any dominant company that gets into the position of being so successful that it doesn't feel it needs to listen to its customers would do well to consider what Gerstner did shortly after joining IBM.

In a meeting with the 50 top executives at IBM, he said he wanted them each to visit a minimum of five big customers over three months. "The executives were to listen, to show the customer that we cared, and to implement holding action as appropriate," Gerstner wrote in his memoir, which devotes a chapter to Operation Bear Hug. "Each of their direct reports (a total of more than 200 executives) was to do the same." Moreover, Gerstner wanted his executives to listen carefully enough that they could report their findings directly to him. He wanted short reports—one to two pages, maximum—about the Bear Hug visits, and he wanted the reports also sent to anyone else at IBM who could help with any problems the visitors had unearthed. (Chain of command was an institutionalized aspect of the IBM culture, and Gerstner wanted to break the chain.) Gerstner wrote that Operation Bear Hug was "a first step in IBM's cultural change." Not only was IBM going to be remade "from the outside in," but the CEO actually was going to pay attention to what top executives did and hold them personally responsible.

The impact on top IBMers was immediate. "Lou came into the company as an interloper, an outsider," recalls Nicholas Donofrio, who ran the mainframe operation at the time. "He was looking for something to rally the senior leadership around." With hindsight, Donofrio reflects that Operation Bear Hug accomplished three objectives: It got IBM back to its customer-focused roots; it provided Gerstner with raw market intelligence and insights on the business; and it gave the new CEO a sense of the leaders he had inherited. The ability of the CEO to gather information alone made Bear Hug worthwhile, recalls Donofrio. "Lou has an amazing capacity to read," he says.

Like "Ben" in the United Airlines commercials, Gerstner saved some of the key partner and customer meetings for himself. He met with Andy Grove of Intel and Bill Gates of Microsoft, as well as Jim Manzi of Lotus, which IBM under Gerstner eventually would buy. By having candid conversations with top leaders in the technology industry—leaders who had the technical skills that Gerstner lacked—he was able to identify IBM's weaknesses and to begin to build an idea of IBM's strategic strengths as well.

Instituting Operation Bear Hug looks in retrospect like an obvious decision. In fact, it helped Gerstner counteract even bigger decisions that had been made at IBM before he arrived. When Gerstner walked in the door at IBM, the company already was preparing to break itself up. It had retained investment bankers to ready initial public offering presentations and accountants to prepare the books of its various divisions to become independent companies.

What Gerstner heard from customers he met, coupled with the Bear Hug reports and his own experiences at American Express, led him to a completely different conclusion: For the time being, IBM made sense together. Owning computing components like mainframe computers, PCs, disk drives, and semiconductors gave IBM institutional knowledge that its competitors lacked. What's more, the mainframe business IBM invented and dominated for years could be profitable again, as long as IBM didn't keep prices so high that competitors grabbed its share of the market.

The most important lesson from showering attention on customers was their dissatisfaction with their IT purchases. In the same speech in which Gerstner famously announced that IBM didn't need a vision "right now" as much as it needed better execution and customer focus, he slyly presented in public the seeds of IBM's grand vision. "We are going to continue to be, in fact, the only full-service provider in the industry, but what our customers are telling us is they need IBM to be a full-solutions company," Gerstner said in July 1993. "And we're going to do more and more of that and build the skills to get it done."

Observers focused on hardware and software probably would have missed the emphasis on "solutions" that day. In fact, over the next decade IBM would shift its entire emphasis to providing high-margin "solutions" for it clients, frequently in the form of lucrative consulting and hardware/software strategy integration projects. It is what set IBM apart from the competition, and the seeds for the strategic shift were sown in the advice IBM sought from its own customers in what Gerstner, never the most lovable of business executives, dubbed Operation Bear Hug. One of the partners Gerstner solicited in his first days at the company neatly summed up Gerstner's accomplishment: "Lou Gerstner has defined his sandbox, and it is a very big sandbox and a very appropriate one for IBM," Intel's Andy Grove told *Fortune* in 1997.

With a focus on its customers, Gerstner also introduced some innovations that are standard practice at IBM today. They include the convening of CIO councils, groups of chief information officers, also known as customers, that IBM periodically brings together to discuss industry trends—and how IBM's goods and services can help customers take advantage of them. Today the company hands out an annual IBM Gerstner Award for Client Excellence to the teams that go above and beyond the call of duty in serving customers. "Ben" would be proud.

15

WAL-MART'S SATURDAY MORNING MEETING

By **HANK GILMAN**

Fifty years ago Wal-Mart was nothing more than a single store outside Bentonville, Ark. One day founder Sam Walton made a decision that changed the destiny of his company: He started gathering his employees early Saturday mornings in the store's office and had them go over the previous week's numbers. What was selling? What wasn't selling? How did sales compare with the previous week? The Saturday morning meeting became a mainstay as Wal-Mart grew into the world's largest retailer, and still exists to this day. The meeting put Wal-Mart days ahead of the competition—and you can argue that it's been days ahead ever since. The retailer perfected the art of learning fast and acting fast, and in the process discovered that you don't have to be years ahead, just days ahead. Here's how Sam came to this momentous decision and why. —V.H.

SOMETIMES A PRETTY GOOD DECISION ends up being a pretty great decision. You just might not know it at the time.

That's the story of Wal-Mart's legendary Saturday morning meeting held at the company's Bentonville headquarters. Part pep rally, part merchandising seminar, part town-hall forum, the Saturday morning meeting was for years the engine that drove the Wal-Mart machine. It helped Wal-Mart become the world's largest company—depending on the year—with 10,000-plus stores (including Sam's Club) producing sales of about $447 billion annually. It worked its magic when the company was a small collection of discount stores. It worked when it became the world's largest and most dominant retailer. You could argue it's the most famous management meeting ever.

It all started in 1962. Founder Sam Walton, a 24/7 executive before they called it 24/7, thought it wasn't fair that the clerks were working Saturdays while the company's executives were, say, watching their kids' Little League games or playing golf. Sam's wife, Helen, felt differently, according to *Fortune*'s Brent Schlender in his 2005 story on the meeting. She believed that the company's managers worked hard enough, and that it was important for them to spend time with their families.

No matter. Sam believed that you couldn't even think of a career in retail without working weekends. That's when a large part of the business was being done. And that's why Walton would spend early Saturday morning in the store's office going over the previous week's numbers. What was selling? What wasn't selling? How did sales compare with the previous week's?

The store's workers had to arrive early. As Schlender wrote: "He'd hold a meeting before the open sign was hung out and share his observations with the whole crew, ask their opinions, and decide what items to put on sale and display more prominently."

That accomplished a number of things. For one, it made his employees feel a lot better about working for Walton. It showed that he trusted them. It showed they were part of the business. It also showed he was willing to be in the trenches with them. That was no small thing. I covered the company in the 1980s and was convinced that Walton and his executives had figured out the holy grail of retail: Keep your minimum-wage employees happy, and your customers will be happy—and then your investors will be happy.

It's one thing to have a small weekly meeting when you run one or two stores. It's another game altogether when you're growing and adding employees. But the tradition continued: Every Saturday, Walton would require his salaried employees to show up, share the weekly sales results, and make plans for the following week.

The meeting also provided his employees a weekly lesson in merchandising. Again, this was at the core of Wal-Mart's success over the years, even as the store became a multibillion-dollar chain. A few years back I interviewed Sam Walton's friend and successor, David Glass. One of the big results of the Saturday morning meeting, he explained, was that it was a way to distribute information about the business to everyone in the company. It helped make its employees, well, shopkeepers. "Sam shared total information with everyone in every store, in every community," said Glass. "He felt we were all partners. He was absolutely right. He believed everyone should be an entrepreneur. If you ran the toy department in a store in Harrison, Ark., you'd have all your financial information. So you're just like the toy entrepreneur of Harrison."

Though it may not have been obvious at the time, the Saturday morning meeting let Wal-Mart compete with Kmart, which was much stronger in those days. In the mid-1970s, Wal-Mart was only a fraction of the size of Kmart, which was considered state-of-the-art when it came to discount retailing. One way Walton figured he could compete was speed. If the battery display wasn't generating enough sales from its spot at the local Wal-Mart, every store would move the display to another part of the store on Monday morning.

"The idea of [the Saturday morning meeting] is very simple," David Glass said. "Nothing very constructive happens in the office. Everybody else had gone to a regional offices system—Sears, Kmart, everybody—but we decided to send everybody from Bentonville out to the stores Monday through Thursday and bring them back Thursday night. On Friday morning we'd have our merchandising meetings. But on Saturday morning we'd have our sales meeting for the week. And we'd have all the information from the people who had been out in the field. They're telling us what the competitors are doing, and we'd get reports from people in the regions who had been traveling throughout the week."

With that in hand, Wal-Mart could move fast, said Glass. "So we decide then what corrective action we want to take. And before noon on Saturday, the regional manager was required to call all his district managers, giving them directions as to what we were going to do or change. By noon on Saturday, we had all our corrections in place. Our competitors, for the most part, got their sales results on Monday for the prior week. Now they're 10 days behind, and we've already made corrections."

That was no small thing. You can argue that the Saturday morning meeting not only led to the decline of Kmart and Sears in the rural markets, and eventually all markets, but also was the beginning of the end of a lot of stodgy independent merchants. (That's good—and bad!)

First, the big guys. As Glass would tell you, Kmart was so strong and so smart in the 1970s that it refused to mess with its formula of uniformity in its operations.

In other words, what was good enough for Springfield, Mass., was good enough for Beaufort, S.C. Big mistake. Wal-Mart, meanwhile, was taking the best of what Kmart was doing, made it better, and implemented those changes rapidly. Wal-Mart executives would then make additional changes on a weekly basis, based on the information they gleaned from the Friday and Saturday meetings. If a lot of high-margin dog food was selling well, executives in Bentonville would make sure the stores had more and didn't run out of it. Simply put, Wal-Mart was a lot better than everybody else.

Its speed and ability to be entrepreneurial also spelled doom for many small-town retailers. A lot of the blame, even to this day, goes to Wal-Mart's power to extract low prices from its suppliers. (Another great decision: Wal-Mart was one of the first chains to buy directly from manufacturers instead of wholesalers.) But the ability of store managers to run their own show and have big-city products all in one place—and at the right price—was what really did in mom-and-pop stores.

The strategy had its roots in the Saturday morning meeting, of course, and the entrepreneurial spirit that the meeting generated.

So what is the Saturday morning meeting like? In the early days it was one giant share-a-thon: Employees touted their best ideas—the famous Wal-Mart "greeter" was a concept developed by a store employee. Some executives would show best-practices videos and use the occasion to reiterate company rules, among other things. Remember, only a few years ago the company was often under siege from unions and the media for its employment practices.

Over the years the meetings became a little stale, and executives worried that headquarters employees would lose focus. To freshen things up, the company started bringing in guest stars, from Adam Sandler to Oprah Winfrey to Peyton Manning. I had the chance to see Gov. Bill Clinton in action. (He answered questions ranging from foreign-policy trade issues to the Arkansas Razorbacks. You could tell you'd be hearing from him again—that's for sure.)

"The point was to make it interesting enough to where everybody wants to be there, even though it's a Saturday morning," David Glass told *Fortune*. "But you had to be careful how you did that, because it becomes more fun to do that than to fix the problems."

The meeting also became a great way for vendors to strut their stuff. Even Steve Jobs, co-founder of Apple as well as the animation company Pixar, showed up wearing his company baseball cap to peddle *Finding Nemo* in 2003. "I love going to the Saturday morning meeting not only because it's such a great show, but because they're really smart and we learn a lot about retailing and merchandising," Jobs told *Fortune*'s Schlender.

Other executives, like former General Electric CEO Jack Welch, would come to pick up tips from the Wal-Mart way.

Today the Saturday morning meeting at the Bentonville headquarters may not be the way it was back in the day. You could say it's now more strategic and broad. The more detailed issues are handled in a myriad of other meetings during the course of the week. And today it takes place only monthly.

But it still helps to keep the company in touch with what's going on in the field and, perhaps more important, making the headquarters and others in the empire feel involved. Meanwhile, the original meeting, or the spirit of it, is duplicated on various days of the week everywhere in every store: Numbers are doled out to staff, and employees have the chance to present their best ideas, some of which may be uploaded to the weekly merchandise meetings.

Or even to the Saturday morning meeting itself.

16

IS YOUR BUSINESS IN TROUBLE? PIVOT!

By **GEOFF COLVIN**

Two centuries ago Eli Whitney envisioned a system for transforming gun-making—then a craft of skilled artisans—into a process performed by unskilled workers. He decided to do business in a way that existed nowhere else. His system of interchangeable parts radically altered manufacturing, allowing it scale in a way no one had ever imagined. Today's managers often get caught up in incremental change. What we learn from Whitney is that when a business is at a crossroads, its leaders sometimes need to risk everything, even before the solution or outcome is fully understood. In management parlance, Whitney "pivoted" from making cotton gins to mass-producing guns. More recent business history holds examples of similar dramatic pivots: Polaroid founder Edwin Land abandoned his plan for creating polarized (thus the name) windshields and headlights to produce the first instant camera—to keep his investors from losing their money. And in the 1980s, when Intel was getting crushed in memory chips, Andy Grove "pivoted" out of his company's main business and switched to microprocessors. Eli Whitney would be proud. —V.H.

EVERYTHING YOU KNOW ABOUT Eli Whitney is wrong, but the little-known truth is enough to enshrine him as one of the world's great businesspeople. He indeed changed the history of the world economy, as you learned long ago. Just not quite in the way you think.

He did it most lastingly not through an invention, as we were all taught, but through a great business decision, a brave, bet-the-ranch decision at a critical moment in his life that shaped the way all products are manufactured, even today, and inspired efficiencies that make modern life possible. He was an entrepreneur and a visionary. Virtually none of that is conveyed in elementary-school textbooks, which is where most people begin and end their acquaintance with Whitney. He is celebrated as an inventor, as any American schoolchild will tell you. That's where the misinformation begins.

Eli Whitney did not invent the cotton gin; his experience with that machine did, however, set the stage for his later, momentous business decision. A number of cotton gins—"engines" for taking seeds out of cotton fibers—already existed in 1793, when Whitney traveled from his home state of Connecticut to Georgia, then a magnet for ambitious Yankees. The trouble was that existing gins worked only with long-staple cotton, known as Sea Island cotton, which grew in sandy soil; most of the South could support only short-staple cotton, from which seeds had to be separated by hand, a process so costly the crop was barely worth growing.

Whitney, at age 28, invented a gin that worked with short-staple cotton, revolutionizing the economy of the South and radically altering the course of U.S. history—just as we learned in school. Yet even this isn't quite right. Whitney's original design included significant flaws, and some scholars now believe they were corrected by Catherine Littlefield Greene, widow of the Revolutionary War general Nathanael Greene. Whitney was staying at her plantation at the time.

Another myth: The cotton gin made Whitney rich. Indeed, it's often regarded as the foundation of the legendary Whitney business empire, which continued well into the 20th century; an indirect descendant, John Hay Whitney, founded the venture capital industry by starting J.H. Whitney & Co. in 1946. In reality the cotton gin nearly ruined Whitney. Though he obtained a patent, cotton growers and processors flagrantly violated it, challenged it forcefully in court, and influenced state legislatures to pass laws entitling Whitney to a piddling fraction of the profits the machine made possible. Whitney fought back, spending more on the battle than he got from it. When he finally shut down his cotton gin factory, he was struggling to avoid bankruptcy.

So here was Whitney's situation in 1798: He's back in New Haven, 33 years old, world famous, and almost broke. At this point in his business career, Whitney made a pivot so audacious it seems insane.

The U.S. government needed muskets. War with France was looking likely, and Europe was such a cauldron that all major nations were hoarding weapons, so the U.S. couldn't buy guns there. American gunmakers were slow. They were highly skilled craftsmen who fashioned each musket individually, producing a few weapons a year, and they couldn't possibly meet the government's demand.

Whitney proposed making the guns by a completely different

method—and here we encounter at least two more myths. One is that in his plans to make firearms efficiently, Whitney originated the idea of interchangeable parts. He didn't. The other myth surrounds a memorable scene in which Whitney demonstrates his idea to President John Adams and skeptical military officials by bringing several muskets to Washington, disassembling them, mixing up the parts, and then reassembling them—and everything fits! The demonstration happened, but at least one scholar now says it was rigged, a stalling tactic to buy Whitney time on a government contract that by then was running way behind schedule.

The real story is a bit less inspiring for inventors but far more so for businesspeople. Whitney said he would do business in a way that existed nowhere else on anywhere near the scale he envisioned. He would produce 10,000 muskets for a price of $134,000. It was a mammoth transaction by the standards of the young country, and it put Whitney at enormous risk. He was now on the hook to deliver those guns. He was almost insolvent and had been forced to borrow the money he needed. And he needed a lot: He had no factory, no employees, no machines for making guns. He had never made a gun in his life.

This was the decision that changed everything. The government agreed to it because Whitney was famous, because it was desperate, and because what he proposed made sense.

Whitney envisioned an entire system for transforming a craft performed by skilled artisans into a process performed by unskilled workers. As he explained in a letter to Treasury Secretary Oliver Wolcott, "One of my primary objectives is to form the tools so that the tools themselves shall fashion the work and give to every part its just proportions, which once accomplished, will give exceptional uniformity to the whole."

The tools will fashion the work. So, for example, he created a filing jig that prevented the workman from filing a part at the wrong angle. He created drilling plates to ensure that all holes were drilled in the right place—and the same place. He engineered stops on lathes so that parts couldn't be turned too much or too little. He built his factory on the banks of the Mill River outside New Haven so he could use water power rather than muscle power.

Each worker would do just one thing. Not make one part. Do one thing. Some gunmakers in England and the U.S. were trying a system in which each worker made just one part. But making something even as simple as a trigger involves several steps—forging the metal in the basic shape, filing, polishing, hardening. Whitney's workers would do just one thing.

The individual elements of Whitney's system were not new. Most notably, the idea of interchangeable parts was hardly novel. How could it have been? It's obvious. Evidence suggests the ancient Greeks were on to it for making ships. A Swedish clockmaker, Christopher Polhem, was using interchangeable parts almost 100 years before Whitney started making muskets. French arms makers were working on the idea in the 18th century, and while Whitney was just starting to organize his factory, Simeon North was making pistols for the government using highly standardized parts just 20 miles away. Historians now believe that true, full interchangeability of gun parts wasn't achieved by anyone until after Whitney's death in 1825—some say at the government's Harper's Ferry, Va., armory in 1827; others at the Springfield Armory in Massa-chusetts in the 1840s.

Nor was Whitney the first to assign workers to a single task in multistep manufacturing. On the contrary, the practice was well established in some industries and had been famously de-scribed by Adam Smith in his *Wealth of Nations* (1776), where his example of the pin factory forever epitomized the division of labor. The idea of using water power was of course ancient.

The elements of the system weren't novel—yet the idea of combining them at large scale in an endeavor like gunmak-ing was revolutionary. Division of labor was fine for making a rudimentary product like pins, but guns were precision instru-ments requiring highly skilled craftsmen, or so it was thought. Ditto with water power: It made sense for grinding grain, but what good was it to gunsmiths, who worked at a bench using hand tools?

Getting Whitney's large, fundamentally new system to work was not easy. He had to build a new riverside operation and de-sign new machines that could be powered by water and could make gun parts in large quantities with high precision. He built housing for his workers. He tried to hire skilled craftsmen, but they already knew how guns were made and didn't like being told to do it differently; Whitney found that unskilled workers were cheaper to hire and easier to train.

His contract called for him to deliver 10,000 muskets in 28 months. The time passed, and he didn't deliver even one. That's when he traveled to Washington for his celebrated demo to the President; he needed a contract extension and got it. He con-tinued to design machines, build buildings, hire workers, and struggle with his new method of making a complex product. In September 1801 he finally delivered a few muskets. He didn't deliver the last of the 10,000 until 1809, 10 years after the contract had been signed. Whether he made a dime of profit is impossible to calculate, but if he made anything at all, it wasn't much.

Yet it was clear that Whitney's new system worked. It was the future. One reason the first contract required 10 years to fulfill is that he was constantly refining the process and designing new machines. He won more contracts, and at long last he got rich.

The system Whitney used became known as the American system of manufactures. He emphatically did not develop it alone. Other entrepreneurs were working feverishly on similar systems, as were the U.S. government armories. Marc Brunel, the famed English engineer, was combining the same elements (in making pulley blocks) at exactly the same time as Whitney.

Yet Whitney deserves more credit than anyone else for the development of this world-changing innovation. Partly that's because he used it to manufacture a complex product. A gun comprises dozens of parts, some of them quite small and intricate, each requiring many different operations to produce. Whitney had to massively reconceive how guns are made, devising ways for each part to be produced by unskilled workers rather than by artisans, designing and building new machines for those workers to use. Guns were advanced technology, and Whitney's application of the new system was its most impressive early use.

Whitney deserves credit also because, more than anyone else, he made the American system famous. His multibuilding manufacturing complex, Whitneyville, became a tourist attraction. Brunel's work in Britain was pioneering, but the new system didn't catch on there until the mid-19th century, and when it did, it was imported from America.

The American system shaped our world in profound ways. By enabling unskilled employees to work in factories, it hastened the migration of farm workers to cities and opened new opportunities for many. It also enabled women and children to work in factories, with devastating effects as the century progressed. Skilled artisans found their skills devalued and their social status diminished. The new system led to another new concept, the assembly line; with the fabrication of parts now separated from the job of fitting them together, there arose a whole new class of factories devoted to assembling the premade parts.

The American system was inevitable. But it needn't have developed as early as it did, or in the U.S. If it hadn't, America's journey to becoming the world's largest economy would have been radically different. History advanced as it did in large part because of Whitney's decision to risk everything on a new production system, even before he himself fully understood what it would be.

17

THE HP WAY: PUTTING TRUST BEFORE PROFIT

By **DAVID A. KAPLAN**

The prevailing wisdom in corporate America during Hewlett-Packard's salad days—and perhaps today as well—was that management's chief responsibility was to shareholders. Founders Bill Hewlett and Dave Packard believed that to be far too constricted. Nor did they want their employees to become archetypes of the mid-century "organization man," who subordinated all individuality to the corporation. Hewlett and Packard made the decision to create a management philosophy built around a fundamental respect for employees. The HP Way, as it came to be called, instilled teamwork, trust, and risk taking throughout the organization and became a template for how today's most successful companies, from Starbucks to Google, operate. In the end "their greatest product was the Hewlett-Packard Co., and their greatest idea was the HP Way," wrote the management expert Jim Collins. —V.H.

QUICK, NAME THE MOST RIDICULED, reviled company of the past several years. Think of the Silicon Valley giant that spied on its own board of directors and reporters, leading to congressional investigations. Or the company that went through three CEOs in less than seven years, each ousted under embarrassing circumstances. The company, of course, is Hewlett-Packard, the American multinational with more than $100 billion in revenue and more than 300,000 employees. If there were a management tome of the period called *In Search of Incompetence*, HP might be the starring chapter.

Once upon a time, though, Hewlett-Packard was an icon of the Valley, lionized for its corporate values, management philosophy, and fundamental respect for employees. Over the course of its history dating to the late 1930s, that overarching ethos came to be known as the "HP Way"—and the decision to view the HP Way as a sort of prime directive governing the company made HP a visionary. Though Hewlett-Packard would make computers, printers, pocket calculators, frequency counters, and other products, it was the way it did things that gave HP its cachet. After all, in the beginning, its co-founders had no thunderbolt idea, not even a mediocre one. Its early projects: a bowling foul-line indicator, a gadget to make a urinal flush automatically, and an electronic "shock jiggle machine" to help people lose weight. In the end "their greatest product was the Hewlett-Packard Co., and their greatest idea was the HP Way," wrote the management guru Jim Collins, who actually worked at HP in the 1980s, in 2005.

The notion of institutional morality was pretty much unknown in American business before HP. While profits and growth were necessary conditions of HP's success, it was the culture that inspired so many other companies in the Valley to try to emulate it. None other than Steve Jobs often remarked that the Valley *began* at HP, and the company was a model to entrepreneurs (even if at Apple Computer Jobs was a totalitarian, secretive manager who could be disrespectful of employees). Jobs had good reason to have a love affair with the company. When he was in eighth grade, he needed parts for a school project. He found a "William Hewlett" in the phonebook and called him up. "Is this the Bill Hewlett of Hewlett-Packard?" asked the 12-year-old Jobs? "Yes," replied Hewlett. A few days later Jobs got a ride to HP's offices and picked up a bag full of electronics that Hewlett himself had collected. (Jobs later got a summer job at HP, where he became friends with employee Steve Wozniak. The two would later start Apple, which in a sense is a descendant of HP.)

In 1998, when I was researching a book on the history of the Valley that became *The Silicon Boys*, I was e-mailing back and forth with Jobs about the Valley's origins. He walked the mile from his house in Palo Alto to read me the historical landmark plaque "Birthplace of Silicon Valley," posted in front of the celebrated garage at 367 Addison Avenue. It was there that Dave Packard and Bill Hewlett in the late 1930s built HP's first product, an audio oscillator called Model 200A (so designated, Packard explained, "because we thought the name would make us look like we've been around for a while").

The HP Way isn't a single set of prescriptions. Rather, over the years it has become an amalgam of corporate principles—originally announced by the co-founders, diminutive Hewlett and Bunyanesque Packard, or "Bill" and "Dave," as they were known.

The "Bill and Dave" part was less a reflection of any particular avuncularity and more a commonsense utilitarian approach to maximizing employee productivity and customer satisfaction. The prevailing wisdom of HP's early days—and perhaps today as well—was that management's chief responsibility was to shareholders. Hewlett and Packard believed that principle to be far too constricted. Nor did they want their employees to become archetypes of the mid-century "organization man," who subordinated all individuality to the corporation.

Instead, Hewlett and Packard came up with a small series of objectives that they reduced to writing for everyone at the company to see. The initial iteration came out of HP's first off-site of 20 senior managers in 1957—two decades after the company's founding. The objectives centered on people, financials, organization, specialization, and community involvement. With HP then at more than 1,000 employees, Packard reflected in his memoirs, it had become "increasingly difficult for Bill and me to know everyone well and to have a personal knowledge of everything that was going on." Such were predictable growing pains. "So we felt it essential that despite HP's growth," Packard went on, "we try to maintain a small-company atmosphere and to have our key managers thoroughly familiar with our management style and objective." And those goals would not simply be imposed top-down: "Bill and I felt strongly that if our managers and supervisors were to be guided by written objectives, they should have a part in developing them."

Such essential faith in the individual was the core of the HP Way. Whether in the first version published by Hewlett and Packard in 1957 or as they were refined in the mid-1990s under a new generation of leadership, the ideals didn't change. "We have trust and respect for individuals," states one principle as written out in the 1990s. "We approach each situation with the belief that people want to do a good job and will do so, given the proper tools and support. We attract highly capable, diverse, innovative people and recognize their efforts and contributions to the company. HP people contribute enthusiastically and share in the success that they make possible." Similarly, another principle stated: "People at every level are expected to adhere to the highest standards of business ethics," wisely adding that "as a practical matter, ethical conduct cannot be assured by written HP policies and codes; it must be an integral part of the organization, a deeply ingrained tradition that is passed from one generation of employees to another." How did such generalities manifest themselves in the daily life of the company? The story goes that Hewlett—ever the tinkerer—came to work one Saturday and couldn't get into an equipment storeroom because it was locked. Thereupon he broke in, got the microscope he needed—and posted a note that the room was never to be locked again. That kind of nominal gesture might seem like pap, all the more so as a company grows large, but it's such acts that signal a style, about which word gets around.

The company assumed every worker was worthy unless proven otherwise. Job security was assumed at HP; mass layoffs and ruthless cost-cutting—*de rigueur* attributes of modern business in the Valley and elsewhere—were largely anathema. According to the old HP joke, the only way to get fired involved a revolver and your boss. During a downturn in the 1970s, everyone took a 10% cut in pay—and every other Friday off. When an employee got tuberculosis in the 1940s, HP aided him not only financially but created a catastrophic health insurance plan. Workers got flextime scheduling in the 1960s. Everybody was eligible for bonuses tied to productivity, a system that turned into profit-sharing for all, which today is standard operating procedure in Silicon Valley. Until HP grew too big, the co-founders themselves handed out the booty at the Christmas party.

Company beneficence in turn produced great employee loyalty—you stayed for a career, despite temptations from others in the Valley. There's a reason HP was known as a "country club," though its charter members were rather folksy characters. At company picnics, Hewlett and Packard served up New York steaks and brew. In 1980, when Packard and his wife invited a dozen visiting Chinese officials to their retreat on the California coast, he realized at the last minute that he didn't have any chopsticks in the house. The solution: He went into his workshop and made a dozen sets out of redwood—which the guests asked him to autograph as souvenirs. Can you imagine titans like Bill Gates or Jack Welch doing that?

Teamwork too—which could be at odds with individualism—was part of how Hewlett and Packard managed. "We recognize that it is only through effective cooperation within and among organizations that we can achieve our goals," states a third tenet of the HP Way. "Our commitment is to work as a worldwide team to fulfill the expectations of our customers, shareholders, and others who depend upon us. The benefits and obligations of doing business are shared among all HP people." For decades "Bill" and "Dave" expected to be called just that, and they called employees by their first names. The co-founders aimed to strip other signs of hierarchy: They opened doors, knocked down walls, solicited opinions from the bottom up, and practiced what came to be known by consultants as "management by walking around." The latter practice—impromptu movements rather than structured visits—made workers feel they were all in business together.

It also benefited the bottom line. According to the HP Way, when ego was muted and egalitarianism was prized, "we achieve our common objectives," which include "growth" and "profits." Utopian though the HP Way sometimes sounded, it was in the service of an estimably corporate purpose. Even so, in the pursuit of growth and profit, as yet another tenet states, HP "encourages flexibility and innovation" in the distinct technical areas it chose to specialize in. The company strongly supported employees seeking to "upgrade their skills and capabilities through ongoing training and development," which was "especially important in a technical business where the rate of progress is rapid and where people are expected to adapt to change." At one point in the 1950s, Hewlett suggested that engineers be banned from doing regular work on Fridays and instead be told to brainstorm—"to think blue sky." While Hewlett's notion of free time to innovate didn't quite catch on at HP as it did at 3M and later at Google (see Chapter 5), it did send the message to engineers to be experimental and not to fear making mistakes.

It helped that Hewlett and Packard had a shared sense of values. Hewlett liked to tell the story about a ranch they owned together. Once, when the area was hit by a disaster, Hewlett called the ranch foreman and said he wanted to offer financial assistance to the community but wanted his gift to be anonymous. "That's funny," replied the foreman. "Mr. Packard telephoned about a half hour ago with the exact same request."

Tom Perkins, the nonpareil Silicon Valley investor who in 1972 co-founded the venture capital firm today known as Kleiner Perkins Caufield & Byers, learned firsthand what the HP Way was—what individuality married to teamwork looked like. Trained as an MIT engineer and then getting a Harvard MBA, Perkins got his first full-time job at HP in 1957. HP typically didn't hire MBAs and the co-founders were skeptical about it. And so it was that the impeccably credentialed Perkins went to work in the machine shop on a lathe.

Single and charming, he spent much of his free time in San Francisco surveying the social scene. During his first summer he dated Ellen Davies, a member of one of the city's bluest-blooded families. At one dinner with her mother, he was told, "So, Ellen tells me you're a machinist. You have to understand we're of a certain position here." He didn't get to see the daughter again. Eventually Perkins was put in charge of all independent company salesmen, then later helped organize an R&D department and jump-start HP's entrance into minicomputers. And Packard made a decision that would change his life: He allowed Perkins to work on his own commercial idea on the side, which became a smaller, cheaper laser and which he sold for millions—and thus was launched his VC career. Perkins never forgot the start Packard gave him—and it was Perkins' devotion to Packard that Perkins cited as a reason that he, as a board member, resigned in protest amid the HP boardroom spying scandal of 2006.

Packard died in 1996, Hewlett five years later. They did not live to see their company hit the shoals—from the rocky merger with Compaq, to the stock market doldrums, to the ousters of CEOs (all of whom had been brought in from outside HP). If Hewlett and Packard had been around, they might've ask whether the company's travails were the result of losing its HP Way or merely a function of the inevitable challenges confronting those who succeed legendary founders. They would surely argue that their HP Way was, and is, strong enough, ultimately, to triumph again.

18

THE SINGLE GREATEST DECISION OF ALL TIME?

Henry Ford Doubles His Workers' Wages

By **ALEX TAYLOR III**

When Henry Ford raised the wages of his workers in 1914 from $2.50 to $5 a day, his move flew in the face of conventional wisdom. After all, laborers were drones, to be paid as little as possible. Ford, however, had come to believe that workers were important assets. Doubling their wages would boost morale and lower turnover. In turn, workers could now afford the very products they were producing. That triggered a consumer revolution that helped create the wealthiest nation on earth. Speed forward 100 years. Companies in India and China are wrestling with the same issue. Apple's Chinese factories have doubled wages over the past three years, giving the computer maker, some experts believe, a competitive edge: the ability to attract the best employees. Apple's moves are also early signs of a China moving toward a more consumer-driven economy. —V.H.

HENRY FORD HAD A PROBLEM—he was becoming too successful. The growing popularity of the Model T was causing him to rethink his ideas about mass production. He had introduced the moving assembly line at his Highland Park, Mich., plant in 1913, and it had worked far better than he could have imagined. The year before the assembly line was installed, he had doubled production of the Model T by doubling the size of his workforce. The following year he nearly doubled production again, but this time he did it with the same number of workers. The assembly line had made the plant so efficient that the Highland Park payroll actually fell.

The trouble was, employee turnover was accelerating at an alarming rate. The dispiriting, mind-numbing work on the line was causing workers to quit en masse. The men (and it was all men back then) reacted to their narrowly defined, repetitive, and physically demanding jobs by leaving them.

Acting on the advice of his devoted lieutenant, James Couzens, Ford decided to take radical action. As Steven Watts wrote in his 2005 biography, *The People's Tycoon: Henry Ford and the American Century*, they created a sensation. On Jan. 5, 1914, Ford and Couzens summoned newspaper reporters to the plant to publicize changes in employment policies at Highland Park that they hoped would improve employee retention. First, the company was reducing the workday from nine hours to eight. Second, it was moving to three shifts a day instead of two, opening up lots of new jobs. But the big news came in the third announcement: Subject to certain conditions, Ford would more than double the basic rate of pay to $5 a day. The 11-year-old company was willing to spend an additional $10 million annually to improve productivity and the lives of its workers.

HENRY FORD GIVES $10,000,000 IN 1914 PROFITS TO HIS EMPLOYEES, proclaimed the *Detroit Free Press* the next day. The news spread quickly beyond southeast Michigan. "A magnificent act of generosity," declared the *New York Evening Post*. By the following day, an army of job seekers that would eventually number 12,000 appeared at the plant gates, huddling together for warmth in the freezing cold. Fights broke out, and the Detroit police were called to break up a developing riot. Within a week, Ford received some 14,000 more job applications by mail. It was a remarkable event in industrial history.

Ford wanted to pay them a living wage so that, he would later explain, they'd have spending money to stimulate the economy. In years to come, intrusive meddling in workers' lives and bloody confrontations with organized labor would put Ford's reputation as a friend of the workingman in a less favorable light. But there was no denying his initial achievement: Initiating the five-dollar day was a masterstroke that paid huge dividends for the company and turned plainspoken businessman Henry Ford into the nation's leading reform-minded thinker. "With this policy, Ford overturned the older robber-baron image of the American big-business man," Watts wrote. "He came forward as a new kind of business leader who sought to share the wealth and prosperity generated by his company."

Although some of his ideas, notably his anti-Semitism, were demonstrably primitive, historians see Ford as a product of the Progressive movement that flourished from the 1890s to the 1920s. Behind such leaders as Theodore Roosevelt and William Jennings Bryan, its supporters aimed to reform government, education, and industry, promote women's suffrage, and prohibit alcoholic beverages. For the workingman, they agitated for reduced working hours, improved wages and working conditions, and a stronger role for families.

Until 1914, Ford had been preoccupied building his young business and didn't have a reputation for being especially generous to his workers. He paid the going rate for labor: $1.90 for a 10-hour day in 1908, $2.50 a day by 1913, along with a modest annual production bonus. But as Ford Motor turned out more and more cars, the quality of the workforce declined. While they may have been happy to hold a job, workers at "Ford's" chafed under nine-hour days and six-day weeks, subsistence wages, primitive factory conditions, and abusive supervisors. The assembly line demanded rigidly defined jobs that had to be repeated flawlessly and required little imagination. Ill treated, the men responded with sloppy work and looked for diversions. Author Robert Lacey wrote in *Ford: The Men and the Machine* that Ford himself had witnessed a brawl during a walk through the plant with his son Edsel.

The most visible manifestations of worker discontent were absenteeism and turnover. Researcher Stephen Meyer, in *The Five Dollar Day: Labor Management and Social Control in the Ford Motor Company, 1908–1921*, calculated that on any given day 10% of the workforce didn't show up. That meant that some 1,300 to 1,400 extra men were needed on standby to keep the integrated production system in operation. With a yearly labor turnover of 370%, Ford managers had to hire 52,000 workers just to maintain Highland Park's existing complement. When the company decided in December 1913 to issue a Christmas bonus to workers who had been on the job more than three years, it found that out of 15,000 employees, only 640 qualified.

Another sign of worker discontent that caught Ford's eye was a spike in union activities. Meyer writes that both the radical Industrial Workers of the World and the more conservative American Federation of Labor threatened to organize autoworkers in 1913. Labor unions were anathema to Ford, and he would hold off organizers, sometimes with fists and clubs, until the United Auto Workers, formed in 1935, brought collective bargaining to Ford in 1941. He had begun to take small steps to improve working conditions, installing a regular bonus system and establishing a medical department to treat workplace injuries. Later he would go on to develop a 20-acre park with athletic fields, playgrounds, and a bandstand.

To put a lid on the workforce churn, Ford and production executive Charles Sorensen conceived the Five-Dollar Day. It came with some strings attached. The headline pay was divided into two parts: wages (about $2.40 per day for an unskilled worker) and "profits" (about $2.60 per day). All workers received wages for their work at Highland Park, but they shared in the profits only if they were deemed worthy. Six months' service was required to qualify. Married men were eligible, as were men under the age of 22 who were supporting widowed mothers or brothers and sisters. All women supporting families also qualified. But unmarried women and men who were not supporting dependents were excluded. Ford made it clear that a "clean, sober, and industrious life" was required to receive the higher pay. An employee had to demonstrate that he did not drink alcohol or abuse his family. Moreover, he had to make regular deposits in a savings account, maintain a clean home, and be of upstanding moral character. Workers who accepted the new wage would also be subject to company rules about how to conduct themselves during off-hours. As Ford explained it, "The object was simply to better the financial and moral status of the men."

To enforce his lifestyle dictates, Ford mobilized an army of investigators that at one point numbered 200. They were expected, Lacey writes, "to make at least a dozen house calls every day, checking off information about marital status, religion, citizenship, savings, health, hobbies, life insurance, and countless other questions." To help them meet their quotas, Ford provided each inspector with a new Model T, a driver, and an interpreter for help in ethnic neighborhoods. It was a radical idea, and it was not destined to be long-lived. As the automaker grew larger, individual home inspections became impractical and uneconomical, and Ford tired of defending the practice. "It tended to paternalism, and paternalism has no place in industry," he wrote in his autobiography. "Welfare work that consists in prying into employees' private concerns is out of date."

Few businessmen followed Ford's example of the Five-Dollar Day. Not surprisingly, there were worries that higher wages would lead to higher prices, with no improvement in the standard of living. The leading spokesman for the opposition was the *Wall Street Journal*. It editorialized: "To inject ten millions into a company's factory, and to double the minimum wage, without regard to length of service, is to apply Biblical or Spiritual principles into a field where they do not belong. [Ford] in his social endeavor has committed economic blunders, if not crimes." Competing automakers were appalled by the move and denounced it. They railed that the labor market would be thrown into turmoil, and they would be bankrupted. General Motors raised wages slightly but was not able to meet the $5 level until years later.

The complaints turned out to be mostly groundless; the predicted inflation never materialized, and the Five-Dollar Day turned out to be an excellent investment. Money was never an issue, according to Meyer. The first year's cost of some $10 million was less than the dividends paid out to shareholders of $11.2 million. Workers responded; within a year, annual labor turnover fell from 370% to 16%, productivity was up 40% to 70%, and the number of replacement workers hired would fall from 53,000 to 2,000. Between 1914 and 1916, Ford's profits doubled from $30 million to $60 million. "The payment of five dollars a day for an eight-hour day was one of the finest cost-cutting moves we ever made," Ford later said. Between 1910 and 1919, he reduced the Model T's price from around $800 to $350, solidified his position as the world's greatest automaker, and made himself a billionaire.

Results from the second half of Ford's experiment resonated: expanding the overall market for the Model T. In his comments to reporters at the January announcement, he said, "We believe in making 20,000 men prosperous and contented rather than follow the plan of making a few slave drivers in our establishment millionaires." In later years he expanded on the idea. In his 1922 collaboration with Samuel Crowther, *My Life and Work*, Ford maintained that "all other considerations aside, our own sales depend in a measure upon the wages we pay. If we can distribute high wages, then that money is going to be spent, and it will serve to make storekeepers and distributors and manufacturers and workers in other lines more prosperous, and their prosperity will be reflected in our sales. Country-wide high wages spells country-wide prosperity."

Economists called it the high-wage doctrine: If a company's profits are tied to local consumption, the amount of consumption should increase with wages and wealth. Ford continued his policy throughout the 1920s, raising his workers pay to $6 a day, and he saw a connection between his policies and the economic boom of the Twenties. "The plain fact is that the public which buys from you does not come from nowhere... One's own employees ought to be one's own best customers. [By paying high wages] we increased the buying power of our own people, and they increase the buying power of other people, and so on and on. It is this thought of enlarging buying power by paying high wages and selling at low prices which is behind the prosperity of this country."

Due to Ford's success, the high-wage doctrine became part of the conventional wisdom of the 1920s. It was a major force behind one of the most significant labor-policy developments of the century: the minimum-wage act of 1938. According to economists Jason Taylor and George Selgin, "The substantial push which would eventually lead to the first federally implemented wage floors in the United States came from businessmen and economists, many of whom believed that high wages would stimulate demand, production, employment, and profits." Ford would continue his policy into the early Thirties, raising the wage to $7 a day in the teeth of the Great Depression.

The debate rages on. Neo-Keynesians like Paul Krugman and

Robert Reich continue to argue that high wages naturally create consumer demand and that a little inflation isn't a bad thing. Supporters of the low-wage doctrine assert that economic prosperity is best served by low wages that don't threaten inflation or squeeze profits. Rising wages, while good for the individual, are construed as bad for the overall economy.

Henry Ford never faltered in his belief in the value of his actions. In an interview in September 1944, he declared his intention to raise the wages of his workers "as soon as the Government would allow him to do so."

"As long as I live I want to pay the highest wages in the automobile industry. If the men in our plants will give a full day's work for a full day's pay, there is no reason why we can't always do it. Every man should make enough money to own a home, a piece of land, and a car." Ford died 2½ years later, but his noble sentiments outlived him, and the five-dollar day ranks, alongside the moving assembly line and the Model T, as one of his greatest achievements.

GEOFF COLVIN

A *Fortune* senior editor-at-large, Colvin is a writer, speaker, and broadcaster on leadership and management. His books include *Talent Is Overrated: What Really Separates World-Class Performers From Everybody Else* and *The Upside of the Downturn: Management Strategies for Difficult Times*.

HANK GILMAN

Fortune magazine's deputy editor, Gilman covered Wal-Mart in the 1980s for the *Wall Street Journal* and the trade magazine *Chain Store Age*, and later as an editor and writer for the *Boston Globe, Newsweek,* and *Fortune*. He is the winner of the Gerald Loeb career achievement award for editing.

DAVID A. KAPLAN

Kaplan is a contributing editor at *Fortune* and adjunct professor of journalism at New York University. Before that he was an editor and writer at *Newsweek* for 20 years. He is the author of bestseller *The Silicon Boys; The Accidental President,* which became part of the basis for HBO's Emmy-winning drama *Recount*; and *Mine's Bigger*, a 2008 Loeb Award Best Business Book of the Year.

ADAM LASHINSKY

Lashinsky, a senior editor-at-large at *Fortune*, covers Silicon Valley and Wall Street and is a contributor to the Fox News Channel. He is the author of *Inside Apple: How America's Most Admired—and Secretive—Company Really Works*.

BRIAN O'KEEFE

O'Keefe is a *Fortune* assistant managing editor who writes and edits feature stories on a range of topics—from science to sports to finance. He also coordinates the magazine's coverage of the commodities markets.

JENNIFER REINGOLD

Reingold is a senior editor at *Fortune* and an expert on management issues. She is co-author of *Confessions of a Wall Street Analyst* and *Final Accounting: Ambition, Greed, and the Fall of Arthur Andersen.*

TIMOTHY K. SMITH

Smith is *Fortune*'s senior features editor. He says he has written about many great business decisions, but has never made one. He is the winner of the Gerald Loeb career achievement award for editing.

ALEX TAYLOR III

Taylor is a *Fortune* senior editor-at-large who has covered the global auto industry for three decades. His memoir, *Sixty to Zero,* was published in 2010 by Yale University Press.

NICHOLAS VARCHAVER

Varchaver has been an editor and writer at *Fortune* since 1999. He won a Gerald Loeb award in 2010 for an article he co-authored on Bernie Madoff.